2004 POE

GW01071862

ONCE UPON A RHYME

IMAGINATION FOR
A NEW GENERATION

Southern Essex
Edited by Annabel Cook

 Young**Writers**

First published in Great Britain in 2004 by:
Young Writers
Remus House
Coltsfoot Drive
Peterborough
PE2 9JX
Telephone: 01733 890066
Website: www.youngwriters.co.uk

SB ISBN 1 84460 508 6

Foreword

Young Writers was established in 1991 and has been passionately devoted to the promotion of reading and writing in children and young adults ever since. The quest continues today. Young Writers remains as committed to engendering the fostering of burgeoning poetic and literary talent as ever.

This year's Young Writers competition has proven as vibrant and dynamic as ever and we are delighted to present a showcase of the best poetry from across the UK. Each poem has been carefully selected from a wealth of *Once Upon A Rhyme* entries before ultimately being published in this, our twelfth primary school poetry series.

Once again, we have been supremely impressed by the overall high quality of the entries we have received. The imagination, energy and creativity which has gone into each young writer's entry made choosing the best poems a challenging and often difficult but ultimately hugely rewarding task - the general high standard of the work submitted amply vindicating this opportunity to bring their poetry to a larger appreciative audience.

We sincerely hope you are pleased with our final selection and that you will enjoy *Once Upon A Rhyme Southern Essex* for many years to come.

Contents

Samantha Daniels (9)	17
Sophie Kemp (8)	18
Nick Honisett (9)	18
Conor Branton (8)	19
Jamie Wales (10)	19
Abbie Wearn (8)	20
Jack Browne-Sykes (10)	20
Amy Amos (10)	21
Jodie Lincoln (8)	21
Shauney Merison (9)	22
Michael Bland (10)	22
Harry Roudette (10)	23
Daniel Hunt (10)	23
Charlotte Scott (9)	23
Jessica de Melo (9)	24
Jade Smith (9)	24
Paige Drake (10)	25
Hollie Briggs (10)	25
Micky Lazarus (11)	26
Isabel Allsop (9)	26
Tommy Pallett (8)	27
Atilla Icoglu (8)	27
Demi Leeder (10)	28
Tommy Pocock (10)	28
Hollie Smith (10)	29
Lisa Marie Burgess (8)	29
Tugba Nazlivatan (9)	30
Katie Dulwich (9)	30
Lucy Wood (9)	31
Annalee Port (9)	32
Toby Court (8)	32
Rebecca Ahern (9)	33
Sarah Robinson (10)	33
Charlie George W Smith (8)	34
Stephanie Say (7)	34
Nathan Pittuck (10)	35
Imogen Kenny (9)	35
James Ross (10)	36
Leigh Harden (9)	36
Kieran Cash (10)	36
Jessica Roudette (8)	37
Katherine Bradford (7)	37

Janan Neirami (7)	38
Hollie Diable (8)	38
Joanne Talbot (8)	38
Paige Wellard (7)	39
Laura Cornish (8)	39
Abbey Hearne	40
Ben Murphy (10)	40
James McVelia (8)	40
Vanja Stojanovic (9)	41
Jessica Dowse (10)	41
David Morgan (10)	41
Sean Troup (9)	42
Robert How (10)	42
Rianna McGillivray (10)	43
Adam Parrott (9)	43
Megan Turk (9)	43
Kiefer Dougan (10)	44
Lily Sawyer (10)	44
Sam Cooper (9)	45
Georgia Eccles (10)	45
Alice Harvey (9)	46
Danny Layzell (10)	46
Louise Ritchie (10)	47
Tayla Ling (9)	47
Danny Fawcett (9)	48
Jo-Anne Chaplin (9)	48
Shaun Fox (9)	48

Darlinghurst Primary & Nursery School

Alex Pierson (10)	49
Lee Stanbury (10)	49
Jordan Clark	49
Ahnya Harpur (11)	50
Thomas Bates (11)	51
Katie McKay Browne (11)	52
Laura Medhurst & Charlotte Hill (10)	52
Andy Chan (11)	53
Luke Macey (10)	53
Shaun Stacey (10)	54
Amelia Lawrence (10)	54
James Morfitt (11)	55

Andy Despres (11)	55
Oliver Brown (10)	56
Daniel Allott (9)	56
Max Ironman (8)	56
Sophie Wade (9)	57
Ryan Sheridan (9)	57
Ben Rotherham (8)	58
Rhianna Gallihawk (11)	58
Sophie Linnett (8)	58
Jamie Reed (8)	59
Conor Shepherd (8) & Chay Pycraft (9)	59
Jack Burns (9)	59
Rebecca Kibria (8)	60
Saffron-Rose Joiner (9)	60
Ashleigh Grange (11)	61
Theo Brown (8)	61
Emily Rice (11)	62
Josh King (11)	62
Danielle Botcher (11)	63
Melody Brandon (10)	63
Amy Harding (10)	63
Deborah Reilly (11)	64
Adam Brown (10)	64
Emma Caton (10)	64
Glenn Manister	65

Fairways Primary School

Alice Batchelor (9)	65
Harriet Walton (8)	66
Rebecca Gibb (8)	66
Kya Morgan (8)	66
Aimee Clouting (8)	67
Ellen Sterry (8)	67
Alice Taylor (9)	68
Megan Seaby (8)	68
Abigail Chalk (8)	69
Lauren Watson (8)	69
Kirby Lawrence (8)	69
Rhian Bishop (9)	70
Nathan Rothwell (7)	70
Jade Whitehair (9)	70

Stefanie Mok (8)	71
Drew Mason (9)	71
Amanda Bowers (7)	72
Rhys Tomlin (8)	72

Leigh North Street Junior School

Liam Hough (10)	73
Anabel Farrell (10)	73
Gabrielle Cohen (11)	74
Isabel Woolgar (9)	74
Oliver Bridge (9)	75
Tom Smith (9)	75
Maia Robins (9)	75
Rosemary Woolgar (11)	76
Claire King (10)	76
Bethan Cole (9)	77
Katie Robinson (10)	77
Martha Hopkins (10)	77
Lydia Bradford (11)	78
Eloise Vinson (9)	78
Joel Severne (10)	79
Hayley Gorman (11)	79
Chloe Vallance (9)	79
Becky Davis (11)	80
Jamie Doveaston (9)	80
Bonnie Lammas (10)	81
Jack Wilson (10)	81
Thomas Humphreys (10)	81
Mary Imbush (9)	82
Miles Harmsworth (9)	82
Thomas Meers (10)	83

Our Lady Of Ransom RC Primary School

Joseph Hood (11)	83
Martin McClenaghan (11)	84
Lewis Healy (11)	84
Keir Tetley (11)	85
Rosie Powley (11)	85
Rebecca Carter (11)	85
Harry Powley (11)	86
Sophie Ashkuri (9)	86

Sophie-Rose Glover (11)	87
Rebecca Pegg (10)	87
William Davis (11)	88
Victoria Tamsett (11)	88
Trevor Smith (11)	88
Christopher Beardwell (10)	89
William Micallef (11)	89
Patrick Wheatley (10)	90
Stephanie Harcourt (11)	90
Victoria Archer (10)	91
Callum Matthews (11)	91
Michael Negus (11)	92
Matthew Netto (11)	92
Myles Shaw (10)	93
Hannah Rankin-Maclean (10)	93
James Smith (10)	94
Carmelina Di Lorenzo (11)	94
Rebecca Anastasi (11)	94
Richard Fernandes (11)	95
Joshua Wagstaff (10)	95
Ryan Trevers (11)	96
Natalie East (11)	96
Catherine Hine (10)	97
Elise Kemp (10)	98
William Cooper (10)	99
Elizabeth Howell (10)	99
Liam Wheatley (10)	99
Rebecca Smyth (10)	100
Jordan McKenna (11)	100
Edward Hobbs (9)	101
Claire Petersen (11)	101
Eleni-Maria Liaka (10)	102
Rebecca Markham (11)	102
Rachel Jarrard (10)	103
Kelsey Hibberd (9)	104

St John Fisher RC Primary School, Loughton

Georgia Colgate (11)	104
Thomas McLay (10)	105
Annie Roberts (10)	105
Aoife Spillane (11)	105

St Michael's Preparatory School, Leigh-on-Sea

Timothy Berry (8)   141
Jack Abbott (9)   141
Oriana Nerberka (9)   142
Parum Cheema (8)   142
Sasha Dworkin (9)   143
Alexandra Morgan (8)   144
Tyra Packer (9)   145
Harrison Payne (9)   146
Amreen Rajulawalla (10)   146
Rosie Shead (9)   147
Sarah Pryor (11)   147
Jonathan Kerridge (9)   148
Charlotte Allum (9)   149
Alex Tharmaratnam (10)   149
Edina Fisher-Allen (9)   150
Georgia Gibbins (9)   151
Samantha Fletcher (10)   151
Olivia Clark (10)   152
Karl Anderson (9)   152
Christopher Drube (10)   153
Ronnie Winmill (9)   153
James Grant (10)   154
Katharine East (9)   154
Hannah Stennett (9)   155
William Todd (10)   155
Alice Stone (9)   156
Alex Capewell (9)   156
Jessica Tan (10)   157
Peter Waterman (9)   157
Jack Benn-Woolley (9)   158
George Goldring (10)   158
Deanna Jacques (10)   159
Bethany Dunn (9)   159
Olivia Hodges (9)   160
Anika Patel (9)   160

St Teresa's RC Primary School, Basildon
Harri-Anne Marsden (8)   161
Robert Smith (8)   161
Loren Campbell (9)   162
Coral Witherspoon (10)   162

Matthew Thompson (10)	163
Jeanette Harrigan (10)	163
Janine Powell (10)	163
Leah Langley (9)	164
Cherise Breward (9)	164
Melissa Kelly (9)	165
Shane Thorn (10)	165
Samantha Hand (10)	166
Emma Viner (9)	166
Lyndsey Roberts (9)	167
Lillian Smith (7)	167
Blayne Cronin (7)	168
Sola Ekosanmi (9)	168
Andrew Baker (8)	169
Marie Anderson (8)	169
Alex Metcalfe (8)	170
Leanne Dodd (8)	170
Raeanne Beckwith (8)	171
Charlotte Bettle (9)	171
Faye Corrigan (7)	172
Peter Murray (10)	172
Katie Carter (9)	173
Annabelle Bottjer (8)	173
Ellis Keogh (8)	173
Clare Hobday (8)	174
Jamie Cook (9)	174
Stevie Smith (8)	174
Henry Green (8)	175
Shannon Thorn (8)	175
Laura Broomfield (9)	176
Katie Maginn (8)	176
Lois Blackman (8)	177
Connie Meddle (9)	177
Sharon Madziva (8)	177
Elisha Dudfield (8)	178
Jordan Brown (8)	178
Akanki Baptiste (11)	178
Joseph Wilson (9)	179
Natasha Magnus (8)	179
Luke Matthews (11)	180
Liam Brine (11)	181
Elliott Tyner (11)	181

Georgina Parker (11)   182
Paige McGuigan (11)   182
George Green (10)   183
Natasha Blay (11)   183
Lacey Dunmow (11)   183
Levi Al Blackman (11)   184
David Odejayi (10)   184
Scott Irving (11)   185
Mary-Ann Iyiola (10)   185
Daniel Fife (11)   186
Thomas Bottjer (11)   186
Adetayo Davies (10)   187
Sean Malone (10)   187
Danny Moss (11)   188

Stambridge Primary School
Kirsty Byram (11)   188
Aliesha Booth (8)   189
Katy Byram (8)   189

Thorpedene Junior School
Lisa Martin (10)   190
Roberta Chaplin (10)   190
Leeanne Palmer (11)   191
Ellie Townley (8)   192
Charlotte Townley (9)   192

The Poems

Cars

Cars go super fast
Cars go quickly past

Cars get all around the place
Beaming out a little face.

It's the headlight for two eyes
Squashing all the flies.

James Golding (9)
College Saint Pierre

My Room

Daddy's
making
a
mess.
He
never
has
a
rest,
but
he's
doing
my
room
which
makes
him
the
best.

Lauren Skedge (7)
College Saint Pierre

Detention

I'm in detention
For bringing a toy
I wish I had
A human decoy.

I would rather be
In the safari zoo,
Eaten by a lion
Or locked in the loo.

I sit at my desk
Through the window a beam
Of light goes in my eye,
I find it's just a dream!

Goodness me! I'm late for class!
I ran downstairs causing attention
I ran to school, up the stairs,
I sat at my desk
The teacher said, 'You're in detention!'

Emilio Kyprianou (8)
College Saint Pierre

Chocolate

Chocolate is yummy
Chocolate is scrummy
It is the best
Better than the rest
Much better than sweets
I gave it to my sister
But she only took a bit
She said, 'Yummy is my tummy,
I really like it.'

Thomas Skedge (7)
College Saint Pierre

Drawing

Please can you draw
A really massive war.

If you are in peril
Then draw a Mario level.

If you don't want to play
Then go and run away!

But please can you stay,
So I can say,

'Why don't you draw
A really massive war!'

Anthony Osmaston (9)
College Saint Pierre

My Little Puppy

She won't stop yapping,
Jumping and snapping,

Playful and hairy,
Excited, not lairy,

My little puppy,
With ears that are floppy,

Cuddly and loveable,
Bouncy and huggable,

Beautiful brown eyes,
Half my size,

She's black and scruffy
And loud and woofy.

My nan calls her messy,
But I call her Jessy.

Jessica Wood (8)
College Saint Pierre

About My Day

I don't like going to school
Even though I like the swimming pool
It's fun to play with my mates
And zoom past on my new rollerskates.

But

When school is over
I take off my pullover
To the car I run
I'm ready for having fun.

John-Joseph Todryk (8)
College Saint Pierre

Chocolate

Milky, silky little bits
Chocolate squares of caramel
Melts in my mouth
Around my tongue
Bought by my dad
As a weekend treat
This is all I like to eat.

Summer Coysten-Gillard (8)
College Saint Pierre

My Little Sister

My little sister jumps up and down
My little sister jumps all around
My little sister plays her music loud
My little sister drives me *mad*.

Nicola Wrench (10)
Crownfield Junior School

What Is White?

What is white?
The snow is white falling from the sky.
What is yellow?
The sun is yellow shining down.
What is blue?
The sea is blue sparkling under the sun.
What is black?
The night sky is black, black as it can be.
What is green?
The grass is green swishing all around.
What is brown?
A bear is brown roaring for its prey.
What is orange?
A pumpkin is orange waiting for Hallowe'en.

Luca Cosentino (8)
Crownfield Junior School

Number Poem

In my bag I have . . .
Ten sharp shiny pencils to write in
Nine new clean rubbers to rub out
Eight red pens with blue ink for
When I write in pen,
Seven peanut butter sandwiches for packed lunch,
Six water bottles to drink from,
Five chocolates for break,
Four colouring pens to colour in,
Three broken pencils small and dirty,
Two curly small bananas for lunch,
One big long ruler.

Bradley Narwal (9)
Crownfield Junior School

Colours Of The Year

What is maroon?
Maroon is the bright roses growing in the field
What is blue?
The sky is blue just like the sea
What is yellow?
The enormous sun is yellow
As hot as an oven.
What is white?
Snow is white
As cold as ice.
What is green?
The grass is green
Swinging side to side with the wind.

Grant Woolven (9)
Crownfield Junior School

Alien

Green and slimy aliens flying in their round spaceship
Going around the world
They're as green as grass
Walking and sliding
Falling in craters
They're walking talking aliens
Flying around the world
There are different kinds of colours
They can be red
Green, blue
Nobody knows, nobody knows
They might be nice, they might be bad
Nobody knows
They might speak different languages
They might be small or tall.

Joel Siggins (8)
Crownfield Junior School

Sunset

A sunset is like the sea glittering and sparkling in the moonlight
It is a beautiful sight.
It is a settled evening or night.
It's a lovely pinkish colour,
When I see the sunset, I just want to sit down,
Relax and watch the sunset.

George Stilgoe (8)
Crownfield Junior School

King Of The Jungle

The king of the jungle is massive
His laugh goes through the jungle
His teeth are fangs
He is hairier than a wolf
He is a big cat but more horrible
He brings animals into his trap
Snakes are scared of him
He is bigger than a ship
But he is the king of all kings.

Louis Turner (8)
Crownfield Junior School

What Is Blue?

Blue is an ocean sparkling bright
Blue is a sky glittering way up high
Blue is a block of ice like a domino dice
Blue is a boat staying afloat
Blue is a car zooming very fast
Blue is bright and crashes like a big ball of dynamite.

Jake Law (9)
Crownfield Junior School

What Are These Colours?

What is blue?
Blue is the waves crashing down
What is red?
Red is a rose with beautiful petals
What is white?
White is the snow soft and freezing cold
What is silver?
Silver is a coin sparkling day and night
What is gold?
Gold is treasure looked after by pirates.

Jay Cann (9)
Crownfield Junior School

Colours

What is green?
The grass is green waving in the wind.
What is red?
A book is red, which you can read.
What is orange?
An orange is a fruit that you can eat.
What is blue?
The sky is blue just like the nice blue wavy sea.
What is grey?
An elephant is grey with a trunk.
What is black?
A bird is black flying in the sky.
What is yellow?
The sun is yellow shining all day.
What is white?
A goose is white swimming in the deep blue sea.

Sydney Goodey (8)
Crownfield Junior School

I Think I Know

There's a secret hidden in the deep hills
of green patios of grass.

> It seems as if
> the bushes
> are whispering
> as they wave
> through the breeze.

I can feel the vibrating
echoes
from the mountains.

You can feel the steam from the boats.

> The fur of sheep
> The bark of trees.

I can sense the country
The mountains.

Tom Sultana (10)
Crownfield Junior School

Snow Is Fun

S now is soft and fun
N o it's not in a bun
O n this snowy night
W inter is soft and bright

I t is soft and cold
S ome snow you can hold

F or when the moon beams down
U nder the snowy floor
N obody opens the door.

Billy Roast (8)
Crownfield Junior School

Colours

What is red?
A rose is red in a flower bed.
What is orange?
An orange is a fruit that you can eat.
What is green?
The grass is green waving in the wind.
What is yellow?
The sun is yellow, shining all day long.
What is blue?
The sky is blue, just like the sea.
What is pink?
Candyfloss is pink and fluffy.
What is grey?
A bunny is grey hopping in the grass.
What is white?
Clouds are white, floating in the sky.

Leanne Radley (8)
Crownfield Junior School

Cars

My car is so divine, it makes me want to shine
I washed it just now
Then it's ready to go.
I turn the key up and down
And put my foot down to go.
It went as fast as a rocket
And up into space.
I saw little stars it reminded me of Mars.
It was a bit of a shock,
Then I hit a rock and had a bad knock.
I turned the car around and flew back to Earth
So that's why my car is divine and it's all mine.

Mason Jordon (9)
Crownfield Junior School

The Mountainside

I'm sitting on the mountainside looking at the light blue sky.
I turn my head and what do I see?
One hundred green and yellow fields waving at me.
I look across the big green carpet and I see a mirror
Shining at me.
I look back up to the long stretch of sky
And the wind hits me like 1,000,000 pieces of shattered glass.

I run down the mountainside to get away from the stampede of bulls,
I climb up the trunk of a tree,
Into the arms of the branches.
I'm safe and warm now.
For I am in my tree!

Frankie Lagden (10)
Crownfield Junior School

Beautiful Country

I am starting at the country
The brush of green grass on my feet,
The smooth wind whispering past me.
The galloping of a wild horse,
The breeze on my face.
The bushes waving to me,
The sunset in the sky.
The house below small and quiet.
The neighing of a lively, lonely horse,
The amazement of the sight of the hills
Going up and down.
As I look down to the green shade of grass
And up to the fluffy clouds above.

Emma Birch (11)
Crownfield Junior School

What Is Black?

Black is the night sky
That comes every day.
Black is a jet-black car
That zooms all the way.
Black is dreadful
When you like the light.
Black is Hallowe'en
But every single night.
Black comes every day
But you never know, it might come your way!

Michael Gifford (9)
Crownfield Junior School

Winter's Breeze

I am standing on a breezy mountain
looking over a reflected mirror
I see . . . I see . . .
A little swingbridge
rocking across the lake
like a boat in a storm.
Ice-cold water splashing up
the mountains like a twister
in the sea.
Strong winds shooting at me
like a thousand bullets.
I look above and I see
Dark grey snow clouds just about to
burst like a balloon.
I hear fish swimming like a mermaid.

I see . . . I see . . .
Tree roots like a spider's legs
I marched along the slippery bridge

And what did I see . . .

Holly Clary (10)
Crownfield Junior School

Colours

What is red?
An apple is red waiting to fall off a tree.
What is green?
Grass is green, blowing in the wind.
What is orange?
An orange is orange, waiting to be eaten.
What is black?
A bat is black, gliding in the midnight sky.

Harry Lee (8)
Crownfield Junior School

The Adventure Of My Life

I'm walking along a brown, enormous bridge
and I can see green tree fingers
waving at me.

Snakes hissing all around me
I'm scared in case they're scared of me.

The bushes are whispering about me!

I see, I hear!
Squirrels in a tree munching on some food.
Owls hooting like the strong blasting wind.
The beaming bright blue sky shining at me.

I see, I hear!
Feeling a little nervous but excited
I'm so astonished that this is happening in real life
It's not a dream.

I see, I hear!
What can you see?
What do you hear?

Amanda Marchant (11)
Crownfield Junior School

My Dog Bonnie

She always wants to play
Her birthday is in May,
When I got Bonnie, I had a smile on my face
My mum wanted to call her Grace
Bonnie's the best,
But sometimes a pest,
Bonnie is brown and white
She has a clear eyesight
I take Bonnie to the park
Bonnie is terrified of the dark.

Harley Sultana (8)
Crownfield Junior School

On Top Of The Mountain

I am skiing
In and out of the fir trees
The clouds feel like hitting my head
As if people were treading on me
Instead.
Birds twitter, twitter all day long,
They sing high notes, low notes
With their extraordinary song.

Ellie Woolf (11)
Crownfield Junior School

My Sister

I have got a sister
she is very, very bad.
Once she wrapped toilet paper
round my mouth, said she was mad.
One night she went to bed, bumped her head
that put some sense
into her crazy, crazy head.

Lily Spratt (10)
Crownfield Junior School

What Is Blue?

Blue is the sea
Bright as can be.
Blue is a feeling
Cold all over.
Blue is a pencil case
Sitting near you.
Blue is paint
All over the wall.
Blue is a sports car
Shiny and new.
Blue is a flute
Very nice too.
Blue are the gills of a fish.
Blue is a parrot copying you.
Blue is a dolphin
Swimming with you.
Blue is a flag
Flapping in the wind.
Blue is a book
Filled with stories.
Blue is a planet
Flying in space.
Blue is a shark
Eating his prey.
Blue is a candle bright
As can be.

Robert White (9)
Crownfield Junior School

What Is White?

White is a polar bear swimming in the ocean
White is pale paint slapping on the wall
White is an ice cream waiting to be licked
White is a lily flower looking at me
White is ivory growing into my face
White is a snowball laying on the ground
White is a laying table what you write on.
White is clouds hovering over my head
White is a T-shirt what you wear when it's hot
White is an egg laying in a bird's nest
White is a riddle setting in a bit of cotton.

Olivia Stembridge (9)
Crownfield Junior School

Colours

What is blue?
A flower is blue
Shivering under a tree.

What is red?
A poppy is red
Standing in an empty field.

What is yellow?
The sun is yellow
Hovering in the silent sky.

What is green?
The grass is green
Dancing in the wind.

Joseph Hobbs (8)
Crownfield Junior School

Colour Poem

What is scarlet?
Scarlet is red.
Scarlet is the colour of the rainbow.
Scarlet is a bright red rose.
Scarlet is a red ladybird.
Scarlet is a field of red roses.
Scarlet is a red firebell.
Scarlet is a nice red cosy coat.
Scarlet is a red radio.
Scarlet is the bright and burning sun.

Scott Sibbons (9)
Crownfield Junior School

Oh Spirit Of The Sky

Oh spirit of the sky
I wonder why you search the sky for me
The far away and your heart near you.
Your heart beats inside you,
The spirit of the sky is the one that lies in you.
The goddesses are with you everywhere
And anywhere you go.

Adam Cox (8)
Crownfield Junior School

Colours Of The Rainbow

Wonderful colours surrounding the world
So bright and wonderful.
But people don't notice how powerful colours can be.
They say at an end of a rainbow
There is a pot of gold
And from now on,
People will always use colours.

Samantha Daniels (9)
Crownfield Junior School

My Dog Harry

The day I got Harry, it was the best,
He was so cute, but sometimes a pest!
Harry crawls up in his box,
But he still takes all of my socks,
When he came to Clacton with us,
We made such a fuss,
He has lots of nicknames,
You should see the bones he claims,
When he eats his food,
He eats it very rude,
When I do my homework,
He comes to me with a smirk,
He is my brother,
I wouldn't want another,
He is the best,
Better than the rest.

Sophie Kemp (8)
Crownfield Junior School

Snow

S now makes me happy and jolly
N o it does not make me cry
O h how I like the snow
W ow it's great.

I think everyone likes snow
S o let it snow.

G rey skies gather
R ight now my hopes are growing
E r' is that white I see falling?
A great load of snow came down.
T his is fantastic.

Nick Honisett (9)
Crownfield Junior School

Amazing Things Happen At Night

The frost was glittering and twinkling bright
Winds are outrageous trying to break an icy lake
Snow is a great white blanket and what a sight!
If it was inside I'd steal it and get under it.
The oak trees have gone metal stiff
And Jack Frost is white and blue.
He has disappeared into the amazing snowman
Magic land.
Because he lives there in winter.
It's like a holiday for him.

Conor Branton (8)
Crownfield Junior School

The World

The wheel of fate has turned
It is now three thousand
The heavens are still there but the sky has fallen
Grass has turned into mud
Mud has turned into slush
The world is a desolate place
All the people have disappeared
It is as lonely as solitary confinement
The world is like this because
It's experienced
Years of horror and neglect
The Earth is weeping, the universe is weeping
            God is weeping
Please don't let the world
Get like my poem.

Jamie Wales (10)
Crownfield Junior School

Rainbow Colours

What is red?
A rose is red in a flowerbed.
What is blue?
The sea is blue with waves crashing through.
What is white?
Snow is white falling down as the night.
What is yellow?
The sun is yellow, and as hot as fire.
What is orange?
Pumpkins are orange lit up on a Hallowe'en night.

Abbie Wearn (8)
Crownfield Junior School

When The Wind Is

When the wind is howling between the buildings,
It's a wolf desperately searching for its lost cubs.
When the wind is whistling rapidly it is a lion.
Roaring repeatedly at a man.

When the wind is devouring the buildings
It's a knight in shining armour
Swaying his mighty sword side to side.

When the wind is furious it's a bold giant,
Marching back and forth.
When the wind is swaying it's a cheetah,
Running at the speed of light.

When the wind is swooping up and down
It's a dove flying gently through the midnight air.

What the wind is,
It's a gentle breeze and it's everywhere.

Jack Browne-Sykes (10)
Crownfield Junior School

Chocolate

Sticky icky chocolate
As sweet as sugar chocolate
Lick your fingers clean
Chocolate
Chocolate doughnuts
Chocolate hats
Chocolate socks
Chocolate
Chocolate everything.

Amy Amos (10)
Crownfield Junior School

I'm Too Old To Cry

I'm
too
old to
cry
tears like
raindrops
from the sky.
I'm never happy, a
happy chappy is what
I never am.

I'm too old to cry tears like
raindrops from the sky.
I used to tell stories,
happy and sad,
I want to cry, but I'm too old
I still try to remember some of the
stories I told,
I can't
I'm still too old to cry
I'm still too old to cry.

Jodie Lincoln (8)
Crownfield Junior School

I Don't Believe

I don't believe in vampires,
Why do people say they are real?
If they were real they would be on *fire*
When they say they are real I just can't deal.

I don't believe in monsters
They are definitely not real
Monsters would make us *shiver*
When they say they are real, I just can't deal.

Now ghosts are something else
They are spirits of passed away people and animals
When people say ghosts are real *I can deal*
Because ghosts are real
My dog died and became a ghost
And how do I know?
I've seen him.

Shauney Merison (9)
Crownfield Junior School

Snowy View

Standing on a bridge looking at the view
I see snow on bushes looking at you.
The shiny gleaming water,
The bright sun,
The snow clouds overhead
Snow on rooftops
The tall snowy mountains
Plain white fields
Trees dead, trees alive.
Breeze hitting me like a thousand knives.
Wind whispering in my ear
That's all that I can see and hear.

Michael Bland (10)
Crownfield Junior School

Animals

A nimals are kind creatures, some of them don't like teachers.
N ewts are small, they're not very tall.
I guanas have gone bananas because they don't wear pyjamas.
M ice are nice but they don't like rice.
A lligators think they are waiters because they say 'see you later.'
L eopards are really like shepherds
S nakes like to bake cakes and hang around by lakes.

Harry Roudette (10)
Crownfield Junior School

Mysterious!

I am in the sea
I see ghostly smoke darting for me,
A golden ball is in the sea,
Glimmering,
Clouds swiftly moving towards me
Non-stop
Mysterious buildings hiding from me
Something is not right
Let's wait and see.

Daniel Hunt (10)
Crownfield Junior School

I Wish I Had A Horse

I wish I had a horse
A lovely one of course,
He could be dark jet-black,
He could be light tan-brown,
I'd ride him all about the busy town,
I'd groom him each day,
I'd give him tasty hay to eat,
Oh I wish I had a horse,
A lovely coated one of course.

Charlotte Scott (9)
Crownfield Junior School

My Family Are Weird

My family are weird
but they don't know
I don't fit in
should I go?

My mum is weird
but she doesn't know.
My mum thinks she's pretty
but she has spots all over her face.
It looks like she's been in a bee chase.

My dad is weird
but he doesn't know.
My dad thinks he can play football
but I think he is too small to play football.

My brother is weird
but he doesn't know.
He thinks he's good at everything
He doesn't even know what a ring is.

Me, I am not weird at all,
Of course I know I'm not weird.
I do everything a normal person does,
Except . . . I dance on the bus.

Jessica de Melo (9)
Crownfield Junior School

White

White is like a cloud,
And it's not very loud,
It shines in the sky,
Like a magpie.
White isn't used much
But it gives us a touch.

Jade Smith (9)
Crownfield Junior School

Bolting Blackjack

B olting Blackjack is my baby
O h he is so beautiful
L oving and never nasty
T ickling our face with his whiskers
I n the field, he's prancing round and round
   the gate
N ever ever thinking of running away
G ently grazing on the grass, he moves to find
   a juicy spot.

B eautifully running, he holds his tail up high
L eading the way we ride
A way and away we bolt on the path
   Away and back to home.
C oming home we walk in the set of the sun.
K indly splashy splashing through the mud and across
   the stream we go
J ack eat his dinner so slowly, with the smell of garlic
   on his lips
A way I go from his stable he has a nice night in
C learing his morning dinner, he finishes his sleep
K indly he waits to go in the field, I open his door and he
   bolts out in the field!

Paige Drake (10)
Crownfield Junior School

Fish

Little fish are friendly
Big fish are vicious
Little fish are as small as tadpoles
Big fish are as big as whales.
That's why fish are different to me.
Big fish, little fish, are all different to me.
Fish, fish, all over the sea
Are all different to me.

Hollie Briggs (10)
Crownfield Junior School

Tower Power

From the tip top of church tower
I see
People are ants.
Ivy is like spiders crawling up the church tower.
In the distance
I see
Valley rock and hill
Every house is asleep
Everything is lying still
I am the lord of the ring.

Micky Lazarus (11)
Crownfield Junior School

Death

Death is like a hole,
Swallowing you up like a monster,
Black as night,
Without stars,
Without light,
Soldiers bodies whom death has left behind,
Felt death, saw death, tasted death,
Beyond the noise, fear and pain,
The ring of light calls for them,
And hope glowing
Inside their bloodstained bodies
As they travel through
The ring of light,
The ring of light.

Isabel Allsop (9)
Crownfield Junior School

Autumn To Winter

See autumn coming just after summer,
From the sun sizzling on your back,
to a cold wind streaking down your spine,
squirrels scurrying everywhere,
collecting acorns to feed them up for the long cold wintertime.

The leaves go from green to brown, blowing round and round,
until gradually they fall to the ground.
Then come the children to play all around,
in the crunching, crunching leaves
that are blowing in the breeze.

Suddenly an icy wind meets the autumn leaves,
they instantly start to freeze on the snow covered ground.
The creatures are all sleeping cosy and warm,
tucked away inside their nests not making a sound.

Tommy Pallett (8)
Crownfield Junior School

A Jungle

A jungle heats up from the beaming sun in the day.
At night the jungle glitters and rustles
From the starry sky with the moon shining down.

At dawn in the jungle the sea crushes and washes up
the seashore where the shells clutter with the seaweed
drying up on the yellow, soft sand.

When the afternoon comes all is quiet
except for the sound of charging cheetahs
shooting into the distance.

Atilla Icoglu (8)
Crownfield Junior School

My Pony

My pony is the best
She's far better than all the rest
Always greets me with a 'neigh'
That's why I love her in every way.

Demi Leeder (10)
Crownfield Junior School

Starts With 'S'

A snake?
A scope?
A sweater?
A shoe?
A sauce?
A sign?
A snowman?
A sock?
A shower?
A shop?
A stocking?
A suit?
A sink?
A shaver?
A shampoo?
A step?
A stone?
A squeak?
A square?
A stem?
A smile?
What am I?
I'm a sausage!

Tommy Pocock (10)
Crownfield Junior School

School

School is great
School is fab
School is sometimes a drag
Sometimes people blab.

Hollie Smith (10)
Crownfield Junior School

Special Friend

I have a friend
Who nobody knows
It's not Sam at school
Not Jim down the road

Her name is Laura
But she's not from these times
She's the same age as me
Yet her life is different from mine.

She has a friend called Lisa Marie
I heard her call,
I thought she wanted me.

I answered her call
And lo and behold
My brand new friend
Came in from the cold.

I thought for a while
What is she doing now?
She might be planning a party
But I don't know how.

So I tried to help
With the ideas that I knew
But things are so different
For me and for you.

Lisa Marie Burgess (8)
Crownfield Junior School

Sweet Factory

I love sweets
I really do
I dream all day of a factory.
I dream of jelly rumbling in machines
Chocolate in chocolate boxes ready to be delivered.
A candy disaster in the factory
It was as big as a volcano explosion.
Then caramel in my face.
Chocolate, candy and caramel is lovely,
But honey sticks and jam cakes are much, much better,
With ice cream fingers.
I dream of a factory with sweets and lovely chocolate.

Tugba Nazlivatan (9)
Crownfield Junior School

Seasons

In winter the frost glitters and twinkles magnificently bright,
Where you can go ice skating gracefully, day or night.

With summer the sunset goes gently down like the wind,
but the morning of day, just likes to stay up.

In spring all the nature starts to blossom
you might just see a baby possum.

With autumn the leaves fall delicately from the trees
If you're careful you might just see a small honeybee hive.

Altogether they make the seasons.

Katie Dulwich (9)
Crownfield Junior School

Strange Pets

A pet is an animal you keep in a house,
But would you keep these strange
animals in your house?

Would you keep a whale so big and fast
Or a dolphin in your house?
I wouldn't, would you?

Would you keep a tiger so fierce and sly
Or a lion in your house?
I wouldn't, would you?

Well how about a leopard cub young and playful
Or full-grown white tiger in your house?
I wouldn't, would you?

How does a shark sound to you with sharp jagged teeth
Or a seven foot python in your house?
I wouldn't, would you?

Would you keep a puffer fish with sharp spikes
or even a bear in your house?
I wouldn't would you?

Would you keep an alligator so deadly and ferocious
Or a crocodile in your house?
I wouldn't, would you?

Would you keep a zebra or a lizard in your house.
I wouldn't, would you?

How does a killer whale sound to you
Or maybe a killer shark in your house?
I wouldn't, would you?

Would you keep a cat or a dog to play in your house?
I would, would you?

Lucy Wood (9)
Crownfield Junior School

The Sea

The sea is blue as can be
It stretches out as far as I can see.
In the sunset it sparkles and gleams,
In the powerful beams.
It swoops and carries every shell it crashes together,
Like a big band bell, in winter it's hard and icy,
It crackles and creaks as the birds fly in the high winter's sky.
As the day goes on the ice begins to melt,
The lovely calm sea turns rough and
            Whoosh!
All the shells are gone
Off of the shore back in the salty sea.

Annalee Port (9)
Crownfield Junior School

Badger

Badger at night doesn't sleep
All tight
Instead . . .
He runs around the field
Chasing a little bug.
Then he stopped instantly
And very fast he dug.
He made a very big hole
Like a little mole.
He is very furry
He is very grey
He's just caught the bug
Hip hip hooray!

Toby Court (8)
Crownfield Junior School

My Favourite Things

F avourite things is my poem
A pples is one thing.
V alentine's is my second.
O h these are my favourite things.
U niversal on telly is third.
R abbits are my fourth.
I have lots of favourite things.
T adgh my brother is fifth.
E ngland's my favourite place.

T igers are my sixth.
H olidays are my seventh.
I have a lot of favourite things.
N uggets is my eighth.
G oing to Nan's is ninth.
S o scuba-diving is last.

Rebecca Ahern (9)
Crownfield Junior School

Chestnut Bay!

C hestnut is a lovely horse
H e dreams of wide open fields
E veryone says he is beautiful
S pecial and full of love
T rotting around his field of dreams
N ever laying down
U nder the dusty hay
T aking one day at a time

B ecause he will never leave me
A nywhere, anytime, day or night
Y ou will always be mine.

Sarah Robinson (10)
Crownfield Junior School

I Love The Sounds Of Christmas

I love the sounds of Christmas
It's here, it's here, hooray.
I love the sounds of Christmas
I wish it was here every day.
I love the sounds of Christmas
Hooray, hooray, hooray.
I love the sound of ripping
I love the sound of tearing
I love the sound . . . Yes!
I love the sound of Christmas.
I love the sounds of Christmas.
It's here, it's here, hooray.
I love the sounds of Christmas.
Hooray, hooray, hooray.

Charlie George W Smith (8)
Crownfield Junior School

My Brother

I love my brother lots
But he breaks my new pots.

My brother throws food at me at the table
But he can't write a fable.

He's not allowed in my room
But he still plays with my broom!

He eats crunchy butterflies
But he always tells *lies!*

He crawls on the floor
But he won't go out the door.

He plays with hooks
But never reads books.

Mum just make sure he grows up!

Stephanie Say (7)
Crownfield Junior School

The Brain

The brain is a legal weapon
You use it every day.
It gives you brilliant ideas,
And makes you play all day.
It keeps ideas in your head,
And they don't run away.
The ideas are as quick as a Formula One car,
racing round a track.
It may seem silly, but I think it's great.
The brain gives your body nerves to move
and gives you the dancing groove.
It gets you thinking
and takes your mind away.

Nathan Pittuck (10)
Crownfield Junior School

Stoat

I am a stoat, a vicious killer
But will not eat those caterpillars
Yet should I see a tasty rabbit
Quick as lightning I would grab it
I am a stoat so sleek and bold
My deadly teeth stand out like gold
If I was poached and stuffed like that
I would be sold like a rare big cat
I am a stoat so clever and cunning
If a rabbit saw me I'd send it running.

Imogen Kenny (9)
Crownfield Junior School

Kangaroo

The kangaroo went to the taxi,
And jumped in the back seat,
The driver went about 50 feet,
He gave him sixty quid,
Then he went to meet a
man called Sid.
He saw his son called Kid.

James Ross (10)
Crownfield Junior School

Roses Are Red

Roses are red
Roses are blue
Roses are violet
Just like you
Because they're just the
Colour for you.

Leigh Harden (9)
Crownfield Junior School

The Snow

I woke up in the morning
As early as could be
I looked out the window
And yelled 'Whoopee!'
And there it was
The snow so white
Thank you Mr Weatherman
For getting it *right!*

Kieran Cash (10)
Crownfield Junior School

Why Do Birds Sing

Why do birds sing?
Why do birds fly?
Why do birds have feathers?
Why - why - why?

Why do fish swim?
Why do fish have tails?
Why do fish have fins?
Why do fish have scales?

Why don't birds have fingers?
Why don't birds swim?
Why don't birds interrupt
In the middle of a hymn?

Jessica Roudette (8)
Crownfield Junior School

The Peaceful Garden

The flowers in the garden
smell lovely and fresh.
In the garden they have roses red as blood
and waterlilies as bright as white.
In the garden they have a swinging bench
as brown as the fencing and the swing
is so relaxing.
The shed as comfortable as a bed
It was like going on an adventure
You believe me don't you?
The sound of the birds whistling
And chirping and chirruping.

Katherine Bradford (7)
Crownfield Junior School

Flowers And Living Things

Roses are red, violets are blue and so are you!
Birds sing lovely, sweet songs and so do you!
Parrots can talk and so could you!
Bees make honey that we eat for breakfast!
Trees are there for birds to sing on!
Roses are red, violets are blue and so are you!

Janan Neirami (7)
Crownfield Junior School

My Pet Cat

My cat is called Ginger
He likes the colour beige.
Whenever I call him
He jumps up at me.
I love my cat
My cat is playful
And loves sweets.

Hollie Diable (8)
Crownfield Junior School

My New Pet Dog

My new pet dog is called Fluffy
She's got ginger ears
I love my dog
My dog is very playful
She's never away from me
But the best thing about my dog
Is she is cute.

Joanne Talbot (8)
Crownfield Junior School

Birds

Birds fly high
And birds fly low
Soaring through the breezy air.

They flap their wings to and fro
And land firmly back on the ground.

Can you imagine how it would be
Soaring through the air.
Flying higher and higher
Up, up, up into the sky.

The breeze flying through your hair.
And around your dreamy head.

Paige Wellard (7)
Crownfield Junior School

The Sea

Can you hear the sea crashing against the rocks?
Can you hear the splish splash of the water from the sea
in your socks?
Sometimes the sea is mad
Sometimes the sea is gentle
Sometimes the sea is calm
Sometimes the sea is mental.

Sometimes the sea sends you to sleep
And in the morning you can jump in
and play about,
but be careful don't go too deep.

That is the story of the deep blue sea.

Laura Cornish (8)
Crownfield Junior School

Flowers

Flowers are beautiful
Flowers are nice
You sniff them,
You *love* them,
You be my Valentine.

Abbey Hearne
Crownfield Junior School

Snow Falling

Watch the snow as it falls,
falling from the sky
How beautiful it looks
Floating softly to the ground
Not making any sound.

How lovely it is soft and white,
Gliding as it goes.
Where will it go? Nobody knows
Will it land on my head or nose?

Ben Murphy (10)
Crownfield Junior School

Sports Day At School

There's no day like a sports day
Instead of doing work, we play
We race
We hop
We do a lot on sports day
We even get to watch the teachers have a race
It goes on for three days long
At the end of the day everyone is tired
Even the teachers.

James McVelia (8)
Crownfield Junior School

My Sister The Vampire

When I go into my bedroom
And look at all my teddies
I find that they've got holes in their bellies.
I know it's my sister,
I have seen her do it,
With her sharp, pointy teeth she bit,
She sucks the blood,
And it makes a flood
My sister the *vampire!*

Vanja Stojanovic (9)
Crownfield Junior School

A Young Man From France

There was a young man from France,
Who really wanted to dance,
He sat on an egg and broke his leg but never got a . . .
chance!
The young man went back to find a
dance
but rather than sitting on an egg,
He broke his leg instead but . . .
Did get a chance!

Jessica Dowse (10)
Crownfield Junior School

Space

The rocket speeds across the endless space
Back on the moon the astronauts have got the sneeze.
On the Earth it's all comfy, nice and warm
When they get home
Another pair of astronauts will go to the moon.

David Morgan (10)
Crownfield Junior School

Sports

In football I can do a kick,
But in skateboarding I can't do a trick.
In golf I can whack it far,
But in tennis it's just too hard.
In boxing I can do a big punch,
But in wrestling I just have lunch.
Baseball is really funny,
But in basketball I look like a bunny.
In hockey I get really mad,
And in rugby it's really bad.
In racing I always lose.

Sean Troup (9)
Crownfield Junior School

My Naughty Toe

My naughty toe
Has two or three teeth,
When he finds mice
He eats them in a bite.
But when he finishes, he's eaten two whole mice,
When he finishes, my toe gets fatter than ever,
When he's so fat, he might even burst,
But now he's twenty,
He's got thirty two teeth.
But the worst thing is . . .
He can eat ninety two mice.

Robert How (10)
Crownfield Junior School

My Big Toe

My big toe is bulgy, red and sore
It all happened when I
Slammed it in the door.
I had to put some ice on it.
But now it's growing spots.
All pussy red and yellow it's worse
Than having chickenpox.

Rianna McGillivray (10)
Crownfield Junior School

Roses

Roses are red
Roses are white
Roses are black
Roses are blue
Roses are just for you
If you will not smell them
You will not know the beauty
Of them too.

Adam Parrott (9)
Crownfield Junior School

My Naughty Little Brother

My naughty little brother,
The naughty little rascal,
He upset my mother,
And made a nasty call.

We do not know what to do,
He has caused a lot of trouble,
What's he going to do when he's two?
Oh no, he's blowing a snot bubble!

Megan Turk (9)
Crownfield Junior School

My Sister

My sister, my sister,
She has green teeth.
Do you think she's a witch?

My sister, my sister,
She's always picking her nose.
I wish she had picked a smaller one.
Do you think she is a witch?

My sister, my sister,
She never uses a bus.
She rides on a broomstick.
Do you think she is a witch?

My sister, my sister
Has just turned me into a cat - miaow
I think she is a witch.

Kiefer Dougan (10)
Crownfield Junior School

The Deep Blue Sea

The deep blue sea is full of fish,
And all the mermaids wishes.
The waves crashing,
The tide rolling,
And on the beach the people are strolling.
The dolphins call their name,
They can't hear them it's such a shame.

Lily Sawyer (10)
Crownfield Junior School

All Sports

In skateboarding I can't do an ollie,
but in football I can do a volley.

Tennis is a great sport
I like the way they hit the ball up and down the court.

Basketball is really good fun,
There's no way you can call it dumb.

In boxing I can throw a hard punch,
but in wrestling I eat a whole bunch.
When I play baseball, I like to hit it far,
After every game I always get in my car.

In rugby I'm really hard
But in hockey I just get scared.

That's the end of my poem,
Our time has run out so I best be going.

Sam Cooper (9)
Crownfield Junior School

My Best Friends

My best friend is Joanne
She likes to watch Pepper-Anne
My other best friend is Hollie,
And she is a wally.

My other best friend is Demi,
She likes to draw a semi.

My other best friend is Sarah,
She is a kind carer,
And last but not least, me,
And I can see the sea.

Georgia Eccles (10)
Crownfield Junior School

Love

I love you
You love me
We can be a couple for ever and ever
He's really jealous
Really, really jealous
I don't want you
I've already got someone
I think of my mum and dad, all the
Sloppy
Sloppy
Sloppy, sloppy
Kisses!
I think of my older sister with her boyfriend
All you can hear upstairs is giggle, giggle
Giggle, giggle, *kisses!*
And then there's me.

Alice Harvey (9)
Crownfield Junior School

The Cat And The Train

There was a cat from Spain
Who thought that he was a train
But now he's in pain,
Because he's been hit by a train,
So you can imagine he's in intolerable pain,
After being hit by that train,
Oh that cat from Spain,
Who was in pain again and again.

Danny Layzell (10)
Crownfield Junior School

Family And Friends

My dad sits on the table eating cheese,
My mum's taking the tortoise out for a walk.
My baby sister is in the washing machine whizzing around.
My brother is trying to be a wizard and trying to turn me
into a toad.
Our friends are outside banging on the door.
Shouting, 'What's happening in there?
You're making a great big roar.'

Louise Ritchie (10)
Crownfield Junior School

The Dark Avenger

My hamster is called Bomb
Hello, I'm Fidgit.
He understands every word I say.
Do I?
Last night he was rattling
I was in my wheel all night.
I was throwing Bomb up in the air
He was flying.
It was not nice, I was crying, she must not have heard me.
Bomb loves peas.
She was throwing stuff at me,
They were green like bogeys.
Last night I fed him dog food
Last night she fed me cat food, mmm.
Bomb can sing
I was crying.
Bomb can swim.
She was trying to drown me.
Bomb can climb up all the tubes.
I'm stuck, hhheeellllppp.

Tayla Ling (9)
Crownfield Junior School

Football Crazy

It's cool,
It's fun,
It's . . . funky football.
You shoot,
But do you score . . . ?
Goal, goal, goal.
That's why football's so great.
Well that's my opinion.

Danny Fawcett (9)
Crownfield Junior School

Trouble?

T rouble that's what I am, my parents told me
R ound the park I go nicking people's chips
'O h no' said a woman, *why!* because I nicked her bag
U p the tree I go, oh no, stuck *help!*
B ut then I fell out *argh!*
L anded on the ground and flat on my back
E veryone got their own back on me
    Why me?

Jo-Anne Chaplin (9)
Crownfield Junior School

Quad

A quad is fun
A quad is fast
But I come in last
I get covered in mud
When I go through a flood
And Mum shouts, 'You can stay *outside!*'

Shaun Fox (9)
Crownfield Junior School

Don't Smoke

Yo, yo, my name is Joe
Giving it, thinking you're all cool.
So forget it, if you smoke put your hands in the air
And it isn't fair.
If you don't care, so don't even try,
For you will die.

Alex Pierson (10)
Darlinghurst Primary & Nursery School

The Karate Cat

As I punch this way and that,
I think about my old karate cat.
He would always put on his silly hat
And do his karate on the mat.
He spread his arms out like the wings of a bat
His legs fired out, like the wings of a bird,
He was on the news so everyone heard.
As I punch this way and that
I think about my old karate cat.

Lee Stanbury (10)
Darlinghurst Primary & Nursery School

Smoking

Put your hand in the air
If you smoke
People all around you don't wanna choke.
(Just say no, just say go).

Take your smoke over there
We don't smoke in the air
Say oh oh
Say ah ah.

Jordan Clark
Darlinghurst Primary & Nursery School

Tiger

Tiger prowling through the night
He sometimes gives me quite a fright
When he slyly licks his lips
Or when he steps on snapping sticks.

Tiger gazing at the sky
Why am I scared of him, why, oh why?
Maybe because of his grinding jaws,
Or even his sharp, long claws.

Tiger can be very lazy,
Or jumping around being really crazy.
When he pounces out of a bush,
Or when I say 'What's that? Shh.'

Tiger lying on the floor
With a thorn in his paw.
I went over to pull it out
Making sure not to shout.

Tiger with thorn out of paw
Now it's just very sore.
He cuddles up and licks my cheek
I held his paw and took a peek.

Why did he dare
To give me a scare?
Giving me a fright
Here and there.

Ahnya Harpur (11)
Darlinghurst Primary & Nursery School

Bob!

Artist Bob!
Baby Bob!
Chef Bob!
Devil Bob!
Evil King Bob!
Fireman Bob!
Gardener Bob!
Handyman Bob!
Independent Bob!
Jogger Bob!
Kite flyer Bob!
Ladybird-squisher Bob!
Multicoloured Bob!
Naughty Bob!
Postman Bob!
Queen Bob!
Rotten Bob!
Spaceman Bob!
Toddler Bob!
Under-aged Bob!
Vandal Bob!
Window wiper Bob!
X-ray Bob!
Yoga Bob!
Zebra Bob!
Bob!

Thomas Bates (11)
Darlinghurst Primary & Nursery School

When Mummy Hoovers Up . . .

When my mummy hoovers up
It makes a roaring sound.
When it hits the floor
All the muck can be found.
I go mad, my brother
Gets scared.
While my cat puts on her silly hat.
She dances around the living room
On her little furry feet.
I join in with my cat
And my dad tries to calm us down.
But my brother still sits there with a frown.
Unfortunately Mummy finishes and packs
It all away.
Then me and my cat
Sit on the sofa
Wondering what
To say!

Katie McKay Browne (11)
Darlinghurst Primary & Nursery School

Smoking

If you smoke just one
You could ruin your fun.
Maybe on the way
To Hell you'll say
Wish I hadn't smoked
Or been provoked,
Lots of children out there
Just might need special care
Cause they've breathed in your tar
Even from afar
Put your hands in the air if you wanna quit
Give your lungs a chance to get fit.

Laura Medhurst & Charlotte Hill (10)
Darlinghurst Primary & Nursery School

So Long, Farewell

(This is a poem to my mother)

I loved the way you treated me
But then you started to beat me,
So long, so long, I've lived with you,
So long, so long, I'll stay with you.
You'll be in my heart,
You'll be in my soul,
I'll always think of you
In my dreams.

I'm your soul,
I'm your son.

I will miss you
And I hope
You do too.

Andy Chan (11)
Darlinghurst Primary & Nursery School

My Dog Rover

M y dog is sweet
Y ucky but sweet

D igs holes in the garden
O h how sweet he is
G oing to sleep in his bed.

R over's so sweet when
O n and on he barks
V ery, very furry
E very day I cuddle him as we're
R olling around crazily.

Luke Macey (10)
Darlinghurst Primary & Nursery School

Pet Spider

I have a pet spider called Ben,
He's supposed to have eight legs
But has ten.
Ben is a big spider
But you wouldn't like to find him beside ya.

Even though he makes webs in my room
I always look at them and think of doom.
When I woke up in the morning
I caught Ben yawning.
Ben was slow and tired,
So we pushed him with a broom.

Shaun Stacey (10)
Darlinghurst Primary & Nursery School

The Defeat Of The Greeks

The neigh of the horses going into battle,
The soldiers approaching noisy as cattle,
The clang of the swords as the war begins,
The moaning of a man as a dagger cuts in,
A bow and arrow shooting through the field,
A soldier sees and protects with his shield,
A blazing catapult whizzing through the air,
Burning all the bodies and blackening the hair,
The war is over the city's in peace,
The people are celebrating in their house of Greece.

Amelia Lawrence (10)
Darlinghurst Primary & Nursery School

My Cats

My cats are ginger, their eyes are green
They're very cute, instead of mean.
You can stroke them and tickle them
Yet they don't really care
And they don't really think that anything's unfair.

They can stand up right, they do what you say.
You tell them to sit they will just stay.
If you try to hurt them, they'll run away,
So you get them some food for them to stay.
They have a lot of cat biscuits, they have a lot of meat
But if you give them too much food, it really is a treat.

James Morfitt (11)
Darlinghurst Primary & Nursery School

Spell Of The Witches

(First verse instructions, Second verse spell)

Light a fire of old ash
Then add swamp water.
Let it simmer till it boils
Then add fried newt,
Frog's liver and
Old crinkly warts off a toad.
Add the Roman's shield and sword
That once he used to wield.

Dead ones arise from your graves
From where your tombstone rests
Come rage
Come do your worst and best
Come we summon you to do our bidding
We tell you to attack Reading!

Andy Despres (11)
Darlinghurst Primary & Nursery School

Rock Star

R ehearsing for the show
O perating with different tunes
C hecking to see if you've got everything
K urt arrives, just in time.

S kateboarding to pass time
T uning in the instruments
A rranging the outfits
R unning from one performance to the next.

Oliver Brown (10)
Darlinghurst Primary & Nursery School

Young Boy Tim

There once was a young boy called Tim
Who has a girlfriend called Kim
He was very daft
And Kim laughed, laughed, laughed,
And their house was very dim.

Daniel Allott (9)
Darlinghurst Primary & Nursery School

A Limerick

There was a boy called Dan
And he was an Arsenal fan
He wore blue
And that is true
He got kicked in the face by Sam.

Max Ironman (8)
Darlinghurst Primary & Nursery School

Happiness Is . . .

Happiness is my baby brother
all cute and cuddly.
Happiness is a baby kitten
trying to open its eyes.
Happiness is a barbecue
with lots of hot burgers on the grill.
Happiness is swimming
in a deep swimming pool.
Happiness is sewing
Making it neat.
Happiness is doing karate,
Shouting out 'Kei.'
Happiness is a holiday
Jump for joy.
Happiness is my birthday
Lots of nice presents 'Hooray.'
Happiness is new boots
Shiny and shimmering.
Happiness is being a bridesmaid
Here comes the bride.

Sophie Wade (9)
Darlinghurst Primary & Nursery School

Limerick

There was a boy called Chay
He did not like to play
He met a friend
Around the bend
And his name was Shay.

Ryan Sheridan (9)
Darlinghurst Primary & Nursery School

Young Boy Ben

There was a young boy called Ben
Who looked very much like a hen
He lived on a farm
That was very calm
And now he sleeps in a den.

Ben Rotherham (8)
Darlinghurst Primary & Nursery School

Lonely

I'm all alone
I've got no friends
I wonder why?
Why haven't I got any friends?
Do you know?
At school everyone's talking about
Who's going out with who.
But there I am
All alone . . .

Rhianna Gallihawk (11)
Darlinghurst Primary & Nursery School

Limerick Poem

There was a young boy from Dundee
and he always needed a wee.
One day he was ill
with a cold and a chill
And needed a warm cup of tea.

Sophie Linnett (8)
Darlinghurst Primary & Nursery School

A Limerick

There was an old lady from London
Who fell into a dungeon
She broke her knee
And stood on a bee
And she was late for luncheon.

Jamie Reed (8)
Darlinghurst Primary & Nursery School

The Hunt

Dark sky
See me
Whistling wind
Guide me

Cold breeze
Help me
As the forest
Protects the sleeping leopard.

So may I be safe
From the dangers that
Lurk in the dark.

Conor Shepherd (8) & Chay Pycraft (9)
Darlinghurst Primary & Nursery School

A Limerick

There was a young boy called Ryan
He really looked like a lion
He went to a doctor
To buy a helicopter
Now Ryan is flying in Iron.

Jack Burns (9)
Darlinghurst Primary & Nursery School

Mystery

Tall as a castle
creepy, gloomy
Fingers long and sharp,
like a witch.
Whistling and wailing
like a harp.

It's easy, can you guess?
It's a tree!

Rebecca Kibria (8)
Darlinghurst Primary & Nursery School

Happiness Is . . .

Happiness is when it snows,
For the sound of crunching under my feet.
Happiness is when it's sunny
to play on the beach.
Happiness is when I'm ill
For the taste of hot tea.
Happiness is when I'm in bed
All cuddled up in my quilt.
Happiness is on Sunday
For a day of rest.
Happiness is clean washing
For the smell of washing powder.
Happiness is at a disco
To dance around.

Saffron-Rose Joiner (9)
Darlinghurst Primary & Nursery School

Snowman

Hooray! Snow is here!
Run and skip out to play
Some children in pyjamas bare.

People making snowmen
Singing 'Hooray snow is here!'
Suddenly the sun comes out
Snow time is spent.

Sally looks out her window
And sees her snowman there.
She sees his eyes like
Black roses in red rows.

She looks at snowman
Standing there looking cold
And glum.

The sun is high, all the snowmen melt,
And all that's left of snowman
Is a button and a belt.

Ashleigh Grange (11)
Darlinghurst Primary & Nursery School

A Valentine's Poem

Roses are red
Violets are blue
You love me
And I love you.

Theo Brown (8)
Darlinghurst Primary & Nursery School

Mum

Mum loves hugs
Mum loves kisses
Mum would really love
Help with the dishes.

Mum hates snakes
Mum hates spiders
Mum hates creepy-crawlies
That are outsiders.

Mum loves me
Mum loves Sue
Mum loves everybody
Including you!

Emily Rice (11)
Darlinghurst Primary & Nursery School

Why?

'Dad, can I go to my friends?'
'No.'
'Why?'
'Because we are going to Auntie Alison's.'
'Why are we going there?'
'Because you need to eat.'
'Why do I need to eat?'
'You need to eat so you don't die.'
'Why shouldn't I die?'
'Because you won't have any more experience in life.'
'Why's that?'
'So you can make new friends.'
'Why?'
'So you won't be lonely
'Why?'
'Because 'y' has a long tail!'

Josh King (11)
Darlinghurst Primary & Nursery School

Miss Wakeford

My school teacher is the best
She's very different from the rest
She is there to listen, there to hear
If we have any problems throughout the year
She's young, she's great
I class her as my mate . . .
If there is a teacher who deserves the cheer
It's Miss Wakeford, she's very dear.

Danielle Botcher (11)
Darlinghurst Primary & Nursery School

Flowers, Flowers And Flowers

Flowers come in pretty shades
Even lovely when they fade
Flowers can be short or tall
Even when they're large or small
Flowers can smell sweet
Definitely not like feet.

Melody Brandon (10)
Darlinghurst Primary & Nursery School

My Favourite Thing

My favourite thing is my toy car
Showing my models and my tractors,
I play with them every single day
In my own and funny little way.

My favourite thing is my reading books
When I find one I take a look
I see them in all different styles
And some of them are very mild.

Amy Harding (10)
Darlinghurst Primary & Nursery School

A Green Dot

A green dot
A smelly tot

A mouldy nail
A giggly snail

A fig roll
An ugly troll

A dotty cat
A lovely rat

A green dot
A smelly tot.

Deborah Reilly (11)
Darlinghurst Primary & Nursery School

Dreaming

I'm dreaming of a summer's day
It could be March or possibly May.
While I sit here dreaming away,
I've only just realised I've wasted my whole day
Sitting here,
Dreaming away.

Adam Brown (10)
Darlinghurst Primary & Nursery School

My Best Friend

My best friend is Amelia
The best friend you could have
She's kind to you
And nice to you
That's what she's like.

Emma Caton (10)
Darlinghurst Primary & Nursery School

Smoking

Smoking, smoking, smoking
Never be provoking
From the first fag you buy
You know you're gonna die.

Say oh, oh, say oh, oh
Just give it up, just give it up.

So give up
And get better luck
Give your lungs another chance
So you can dance.

Glenn Manister
Darlinghurst Primary & Nursery School

Holding The Baby

I had gone to my aunty's house for the day,
                                    when I held Lilly.
I sat on the chair in the living room
And hoped it would be over soon.

My parents felt a bit worried
They told me afterwards
But I could definitely tell
That they were happy as well.

I think that Lilly was cosy
Lying in my arms
She was a bit chubby
She's always a bit grubby.

Alice Batchelor (9)
Fairways Primary School

Summer

This is our summer place
And all the trees are full of little creatures
All the leaves are bright green
And the river that we paddle in
Is a beautiful light blue.

The air is warm and smells of fresh flowers
Our voices shout and laugh happily
And everything is a beautiful colour.

Harriet Walton (8)
Fairways Primary School

Gran Poem

My gran is as funny as a chimpanzee
Her hair is like a furry sheep
Her eyes are like a fish staring
Her face is like a wrinkled bag
When she walks she is like an old lady
When she sits she is like a funny old teddy bear
When she laughs she is like a chimpanzee
When she sleeps, she is like a tiger when she snores.

Rebecca Gibb (8)
Fairways Primary School

The Visible Beast

His fur is as black as ebony
His slobber is dripping from his fangs
His mouth is like a tunnel when he opens it
His eyes are like car headlamps
His ears are like tips of knives
His rough muscles pop out when he's ready to fight.

Kya Morgan (8)
Fairways Primary School

My Hamster

My hamster is fluffy and makes no sound
But on her wheel she runs round and round,
Squeak, squeak, squeak around she goes all night
Then she stops when morning comes and it is light,
Off to sleep she now goes . . .
In the fluffy cotton wool she burrows her nose.
Then it's breakfast and time for a bath,
Then off to bed again oh what a laugh.

She always knows when it's evening again,
Because she hears the news at ten!

Aimee Clouting (8)
Fairways Primary School

Flash The Fish

Flash the fish
Swims fast
Faster than lightning
Dashes and darts
Through the cave
In his glass tank
He is as orange as an orange
He's very greedy
He loves to eat
But he's clever too
He follows my fingers
Against the glass
He's the best fish in the world.

Ellen Sterry (8)
Fairways Primary School

My Baby Cousin

My mum wants a photo
With me and James.
I was happy
Because he is cute.
When I hold James
He is happy.
He is only one year old.
When the photo is finished
James is crying.

Alice Taylor (9)
Fairways Primary School

Summer

My job is to make the sun shine
And flowers to look beautiful
I am not showing off
Like my sister Madam Spring
But I am the prettiest of them all

I am the best season of them all
Well that is what I think anyway
And people love to sunbathe
I am not showing off
Like my sister Madam Spring
And children love to come out and play.

People go to lovely places
Which are so much fun
I am not showing off
Like my sister Madam Spring
But people cannot wait
For another day of fun
It is like a holiday!
Yes you know I am the beautiful summer.

Megan Seaby (8)
Fairways Primary School

The Eagle

The eagle large and mean,
Strong and mighty,
His claws are sharp
To pick up his prey
With a hooked beak
It swoops down to catch his prey
And eats it with pride
Then he flies away to another place.

Abigail Chalk (8)
Fairways Primary School

The Eagle

The eagle sits so still on a slippery rock
And tries to find a soft grey mouse,
And suddenly a mouse comes scurrying by,
And the eagle jumps off his rock and brings it to his house.

Then suddenly to his delight
A vole comes rushing by,
And out jumps the eagle and gets his prey,
And perhaps he will go hunting another day.

Lauren Watson (8)
Fairways Primary School

Holding My Brother

My mum said I could hold him,
My brother so sleek, soft and warm,
They said be ever so careful with him,
His head dropped in my arms,
I put his head back on my shoulder again
He felt soft and warm
Smile they said
My brother smiled as well,
My family said it was *great*.

Kirby Lawrence (8)
Fairways Primary School

Winter

W inter has arrived
 I ce glittering on the rooftops
N ight comes quickly
T oo cold to play outside
E veryone drinking hot chocolate
R elaxing by the fireside.

Rhian Bishop (9)
Fairways Primary School

Lost In The Zoo

Where is my mum and dad?
Animals have been let out
People are slipping over banana peel
Lions running around saying, 'Roar'
Dolphins splashing around in a pool
Elephants eating leaves off a tree
There you are Mum and Dad
I've been looking all over for you!

Nathan Rothwell (7)
Fairways Primary School

Rosie The Rabbit

Rosie is my rabbit
She is grey and fluffy
Her tail is like cotton wool
She lives in the garden
She jumps up and down
She jumps in my swing
And wriggles about
Until the swing starts to move
She is really sick.

Jade Whitehair (9)
Fairways Primary School

Neighbourhood Pets

Mr Morse had a black and white horse
Which he brought to his college course.
Mrs Shug had a slimy slug,
Which when she was drinking tea slithered
into her mug.
Mr Beagle had a golden eagle,
But keeping it was illegal.
Mrs Splode had a slippery toad,
That ate too much and started to explode.
Mr Slabbit had a floppy-eared rabbit,
That had a very awful habit.
Mrs Lee had a buzzing bumblebee
Which one day got stuck in an apple tree.
Mr Drake had a rattlesnake
Which one day broke his garden rake.
Mrs Splog had a spotty dog,
Which one night got lost in the fog.

Stefanie Mok (8)
Fairways Primary School

The Visible Beast

In the darkness of night
A yellow beast with teeth like knives
Two fiery red eyes
Roars like a dragon
Eats anyone that enters his big cave
Runs on three legs
Wings on each of his four arms
A head like a bat
And big eyes
Be warned it creeps up behind you
And eats you!

Drew Mason (9)
Fairways Primary School

The Scary Woods

Something was howling in the woods
I could hear it from my bedroom.
Calm down I said to myself.
Argh the wind's blowing the trees.
Rain's pitter-pattering on my bedroom window
Yap yap went a dog
I looked out of my window and ran to my
Mum and Dad's room
Now I felt safe.

Amanda Bowers (7)
Fairways Primary School

The Visible Beast

I was walking through the forest
I heard a strange noise
There was nothing
Suddenly I felt breathing down my neck
I turned
There was a monster
With teeth like swords
A head as big as a lion
A funny body
Ginormous
I was scared
I ran
He was just behind me
I was too afraid to scream
My body was frozen
I didn't know what to do
I tried to run
He followed me
I saw the way out
The sun reflected in his eyes
The monster was scared not me.

Rhys Tomlin (8)
Fairways Primary School

Postcard Home

The magnificent road that inspires great events.
The meandering canal that glistens in the brilliant summer sun.
The heavenly beach that is a minute drop of sun on the shores
of tranquillity.
The trees that bend to greet you as you pass in a jovial manner.
The wonderful creatures that are like huge smiles and a cheery face.
The refreshing beverages that soothe the soul and flood your
senses with a satisfaction so great you will long to be controlled
by its happiness.
Oh! I wish you were here with me!

Liam Hough (10)
Leigh North Street Junior School

A Postcard From The Amazon

Each morning I wake to the placid melody of the stream,
As it trickles exuberantly down to a shaded pool.
The trees seem to step aside to let you pass,
And the tropical birds guide you on your way.
But this differs at night . . .
The dreamland shatters and becomes a danger zone,
Its warning signs ripped down by creatures,
Possessed by the night's spirits.
The tranquil charm is blown away as if it were a neglected cobweb.
Doom awaits every wanderer led astray by the haunting chants
of lethal tribes
And the whoosh of a poison dart
As it streaks past your ear.
The mangled, gnarled faces of the trees,
The glinting villainous eyes of mysterious predators.
     These are the terrors of the Amazonian
     Rainforest.

Anabel Farrell (10)
Leigh North Street Junior School

A Postcard Poem

(For my brother James Hayhurst)

In a place where tranquil waters stream
Where every step feels like a dream
You can hear the call of birds
Whose bright colours blaze,
Like red-hot lava in a volcano,
On a sweltering summer's day,
Where children are safe to run and play.
The exotic taste of spices sweet
Cold ice cream for us,
Just as a treat.
The fabrics feel so smooth and light,
Juicy fruits so soft to bite.
The salty sea air swirls all around,
I feel that I have finally found,
A perfect place,
With no trace,
Of hate, sorrow or greed.

Gabrielle Cohen (11)
Leigh North Street Junior School

A Postcard From Paris

The immense structure towers over the small world,
and its pinnacle disappears into the low, fibrous clouds
that cover the night sky.
Perfumed lights glow as the fumes assail your nose
The food tickles my tastebuds,
Voices of mystery address each other,
Rough metal sends shivers running down my bony spine
And I wish you were here with me.

Isabel Woolgar (9)
Leigh North Street Junior School

The Moon's A Girl!

I had a trip to the moon
It was a fairly nice place
But from far away
It had a very ugly face!

I had to leave early
I was feeling sick
The craters were so bumpy,
I'd had enough of it!

Oliver Bridge (9)
Leigh North Street Junior School

Spain

Here in sunny Spain
the turquoise sea glistens in the sunshine
the fine sand slips through my fingers
like a flowing waterfall.

The amber sunset glowing in the sky
The jagged towering cliff
Guarding the beach.

I love it here.

Tom Smith (9)
Leigh North Street Junior School

New Zealand

The emerald trees sway in the lilac sunset.
The jagged mountains towering over us all.
Lakes with aqua-blue water trickling over a waterfall.
Miles of flat muddy marshes.
Rocks taller than hills
Wild horses galloping over open fields
I wish you were here.

Maia Robins (9)
Leigh North Street Junior School

The Senses Of France

The atmosphere is as interesting as a poet's beginning.
The leaves of the trees seem to bow when we walk past.
The night sky is as warm as the double blankets on a bed
near a crackling fire.
The Eiffel Tower, as huge as a rock to an ant.

I hear the language as clear as a crystal
I feel my hair brushing in and out of my face in the light breeze.
I see the expressions on the petals of a plant, each one happy
and cheerful.
I taste the scent of the roses each one crisp and welcoming.

These are the senses of France.

Rosemary Woolgar (11)
Leigh North Street Junior School

Snow Falls

Snow falls tonight
Soft and white as ever,
Whooshing and whizzing,
In the winter breeze.

Snow falls tonight
I'm really excited
Can't wait for the morning to come,
Snow falls tonight,
On the glowing white Alps.

Snow falls tonight
Wish you were here.

Claire King (10)
Leigh North Street Junior School

A Postcard From France

The beautiful chrome sunsets that I watch from a small
bench on top of a grassy hill.
The taste of a refreshing drink that runs down my throat.
The shattering touch of the spiky emerald grass.
The eerie sound of the wavy ocean splashing on to the seashore.
The smell of the fresh bread that they sell in the market.
Wish you were here.

Bethan Cole (9)
Leigh North Street Junior School

Postcard From India

People dancing to booming loud music,
Camels towering over me like lava coming out of a volcano.
Dresses flowing around me like fire in a blowing air,
Spices pushing my mouth to them.
The water near my ears is like a baby crying
It's so quiet.
My ears are filled with the loud music
Oh I do wish you were here.

Katie Robinson (10)
Leigh North Street Junior School

Jamaica

The clear aqua ocean
And the soft, white sand
Tropical birds singing
Palm trees blowing softly
The scarlet and orange horizon
Is beautiful.

    Wish you were here to
    Share it with me.

Martha Hopkins (10)
Leigh North Street Junior School

A Postcard Home

This place is Heaven, you should come some day
It's as colourful as a tropical bird,
With clear flowing rivers.
You can get ice creams of every flavour and colour.
The sky is filled with big, white fluffy clouds like a
big, bouncy, warm quilt.
The sun spreads hot rays of sunlight, on the fresh green grass
With deep yellow daffodils dotted around.
The beach nearby has sand as rich as gold
And the sea, a big sparkling glitter pool,
With dolphins jumping out with smiling faces.

Lydia Bradford (11)
Leigh North Street Junior School

Canada

Canada lovely and hot
The sea like glistening aqua-blue glass
The sand, soft and golden
The ripples in the sea like grey cantering horses.

Canada lovely and calm
The sunset red, ruby, orange and crimson,
The sun so bright it burns the sky,
Peacock and sapphire.

Canada is a lovely place - I think I'll stay.

Eloise Vinson (9)
Leigh North Street Junior School

Calm Winds

The emerald grass,
The sapphire sea,
As I write,
The cliffs are towering over me.

The ruby sunset I see in my eye,
Makes me feel so happy inside.

The majestic trees whistle in the calm wind

I wish so much that you were here with me.

Joel Severne (10)
Leigh North Street Junior School

Postcard Home

Dear Home,
The weather here is as hot as a flame,
The sky is bluer than the bluest ocean.
The waterfall is a sparkling sapphire.
Colourful, tropical plants in every corner.
All you can smell is exotic fruits.
The peaceful sounds of water lapping.
Soft flower petals stroke against my face
As I walk through the island.
    Lots of Love

Hayley Gorman (11)
Leigh North Street Junior School

A Postcard From Costa Blanca

The sea is as calm as the still wind,
I listen carefully and hear a flock of birds,
I reach out and touch the cream sand,
A waft of dry taste of mussels,
Only one day to go, I might stay a bit longer.

Chloe Vallance (9)
Leigh North Street Junior School

Hawaii

Coconuts fall on every sandy shore
The smell of sea and pineapples reach my nose
People wear grass skirts in the blazing hot sun
I love Hawaii as warm wind blows.

Girls in grass skirts do the hula-hula
Exotic fruits hang in tropical trees
The multicoloured parrots fly around
Calm shores with refreshing seas.

Leaves in the palm trees explode
The sun is like a bit of treasure in the sky
I walk along the beach with soft sand between my toes
As the tropical birds fly by.

I can hear the waves
And the smell of lemon and lime.
I adore watching the monkey in the trees
I'm having a really exciting time.

Becky Davis (11)
Leigh North Street Junior School

A Postcard From Mexico

I smell,
Crispy dry cacti
On a bright summer's day.
I taste,
Several spices are fragrancing the air.
I pressed my hand against a rough temple.
I see,
Dusty bread that people are eating.
I hear
Mysterious voices speaking quietly.

Jamie Doveaston (9)
Leigh North Street Junior School

A Postcard From Mallorca

The refreshing pure air holds the delicious smell of paella.
Water trickles through my burnt separate hands,
The moon is floating like a pound coin
Sinking to the bottom of a deep sea.
The voices of contented birds fill my ears.
I can taste the gorgeous middle of a watering melon,
sliding down the inside of my throat.

A land of exotic fragrances!

Bonnie Lammas (10)
Leigh North Street Junior School

Postcard From The Caribbean

The huge palm tree swaying in the wind.
The luxurious sand falls through my soft hand
The salty air flowing up my nose
The clear cobalt sea as still as a rock
I smell fragrant juicy coconuts fall upon the sand.

Paradise.

Jack Wilson (10)
Leigh North Street Junior School

Antarctica

Cold polar icebergs rise majestically
Penguins float like liferafts on a cobalt sea,
Furry newborn chirping at the sight of day,
Icy air nuzzles my face,
Hot chocolate trickles down my throat,
The land of coldness, ice and snow.

Thomas Humphreys (10)
Leigh North Street Junior School

From Venice

The azure canals glint in the dazzling moonlight
as I run my scorching fingers
through the chilly water.
The fragrance of tropical wines
fills the air,
and tender tangerines silky
as the mellifluous skin of an adorable baby.
The sound of sapphire water trickling
into a slim, shiny glass.

Mary Imbush (9)
Leigh North Street Junior School

The Great Time

The sapphire sea glistening as the waves rush by.
The emerald seaweed lying cold and wet sinking on the Earth.
The peach-sand being pushed back and forth.
The smooth pebbles, wet and dry, pushed in the deep amber sand.
The aqua sky silent, calm and still,
The beautiful flowers standing waving their heads,
As the gentle breeze brushes them left and right.
The mountain tops groan as people stroll up and down.
The rough palm trees dazzling in the warm air.

See you soon.

Miles Harmsworth (9)
Leigh North Street Junior School

A Postcard From New Delhi

The aroma of curry floats in the air
The dusty dry ground
Cory-orts my hand, the golden palace glistens
In front of the burning sun.
The sizzling rice over the fire with colourful spices,
Vanilla fills the streets
You catch its scent travelling on the breeze
This is India.

Thomas Meers (10)
Leigh North Street Junior School

The Scientist

There was a mad scientist
He was bottom of the list,
He wanted to be top
When his brain began to pop.

He began to lack and cheat
And was running low on meat,
He got visited by a witch
Because you know he's mad,
And jumped into a ditch.

He made a special potion
It was called sunny lotion,
Gave it to his friend
And his life began to end.

Joseph Hood (11)
Our Lady Of Ransom RC Primary School

Mac Snow

Who dances low
To and fro?
Mac Snow.

Who do you see fall
Then outside you quickly go?
Mac Snow.

Who gets in your shoes
Then inside you want to go?
Mac Snow.

Who comes and goes
And stops traffic flow?
Mac Snow.

Who do children long to see come
And hate to see go?
Mac Snow.

Martin McClenaghan (11)
Our Lady Of Ransom RC Primary School

Mac Knight

Who fights in battle
At the fiery night?
Mac Knight.

Who goes white
In the middle of the fight?
Mac Knight.

Who turns dark
In the light?
Mac Knight.

Lewis Healy (11)
Our Lady Of Ransom RC Primary School

A Shark

A silent stalker
A sharp-toothed hulk
A blood sniffer
A seal-eating bulk
A dangerous predator
A keen viewer
A biting surprise
A wonder of the sea.

Keir Tetley (11)
Our Lady Of Ransom RC Primary School

Rose Rain

Small glittery crystal beads,
Colourful sparkly flowers she feeds,
Turns a cobweb into a chain of silky pearls,
Turns a puddle to silver swirls,
Sometimes can cause a shimmering rainbow,
Sweet singing birds take a shower,
Rose Rain has all the power.

Rosie Powley (11)
Our Lady Of Ransom RC Primary School

Gone With A Breeze

There was a young lady called Heather,
Who weighed just the same as a feather,
She went walking one day,
When she just blew away,
Which wasn't exceedingly clever.

Rebecca Carter (11)
Our Lady Of Ransom RC Primary School

Freddy Lightning

Who hides in the clouds,
And then quickly jumps out striking,
Freddy Lightning.

Who hits you by surprise,
When he runs along the clouds fighting,
Freddy Lightning.

Who brightens the night,
And colours the clouds brightening,
Freddy Lightning.

Harry Powley (11)
Our Lady Of Ransom RC Primary School

Weather

It makes me very hot,
But playing games is fun,
We get it in the summer,
It's what we call the sun!

We get it very often,
It can be quite a pain,
It gets us all very wet,
It's what we call rain!

This weather falls in winter,
On our sledges, 'Here we go!'
It's cold and white and fluffy,
It's what we call snow!

Sophie Ashkuri (9)
Our Lady Of Ransom RC Primary School

The Last Battle

Battle is blood and death
Battle is hatred and disgust
Battle is brave and noble
Battle is broad metal blades
Battle is heroic men going to fight
Battle is war.

Battle is people landing on their swords
Battle is cold stone graves
Battle is planning and getting ready
Battle is victory
Battle is defeat
Battle is war.

Sophie-Rose Glover (11)
Our Lady Of Ransom RC Primary School

Mac Rain

Everyone stops to complain
In the lane
Who is it?
Mac Rain.

It can hurt the brain
And it will come again!
Who is it?
Mac Rain.

The rain can stain
Who can we blame
Who is it?
Mac Rain.

Rebecca Pegg (10)
Our Lady Of Ransom RC Primary School

Friends

F riends are forgiving and forever,
R eliable and together
I ncredible is what they are
E verlasting so that we'll go far
N ice and notable wherever they are
D ependable or inseparable be at school or in the car
S uper not to mention satisfying
H opeful and helpful not denying
I ntriguing and interesting without lying
P olite is all that friends are.

William Davis (11)
Our Lady Of Ransom RC Primary School

Kennings

A thin body
A swift mover
A camouflaged body
A quick slider
A sharp eye
A loud hisser
A painful venom
A forked tongue.

Victoria Tamsett (11)
Our Lady Of Ransom RC Primary School

A Peasant Haiku

Forcing himself on
A peasant gathering twigs
Somehow he survives.

Trevor Smith (11)
Our Lady Of Ransom RC Primary School

A Friendship Poem

Friends are good
Friends are not bad
Friends make you happy when you are sad.

Friends will always be beside you
Friends will share
Friends will care.

Friends are always always there,
Friends are forever,
Friends always work together.

Friends are never ever arguing together,
Friends are always nice and kind,
Until the day is over.

Christopher Beardwell (10)
Our Lady Of Ransom RC Primary School

Mac Hail

Who hit you
Hard as a nail?
Mac Hail.

Who hits your
Dog or cat on the tail?
Mac Hail.

Who hits you
And makes you fail?
Mac Hail.

Who hits the water
And disturbs a whale?
Mac Hail.

William Micallef (11)
Our Lady Of Ransom RC Primary School

Will Sun

Who will melt
all the snow
when he will come?
Will Sun.

Who will give us
great fun?
Will Sun.

Who will dry
all the washing up
for my mum?
Will Sun.

Who will allow
us to eat our
bun in the sun.
Will Sun.

Patrick Wheatley (10)
Our Lady Of Ransom RC Primary School

A Friend

A friend you can rely on
A friend you can trust
A friend everlasting and will make you laugh.

A friend is very special
A friend is very kind
A friend is always there for you at the best and
worst of times
A friend is always there for you to help you on
your way.

Stephanie Harcourt (11)
Our Lady Of Ransom RC Primary School

Fran Snow

Who goes in the wood at night
And runs to and fro?
Fran Snow.

Who is as soft as a ghost
And blow after blow?
Fran Snow.

Who is by our side all day,
But we will never know?
Fran Snow.

Who will we welcome but,
Only to see he might go?
Fran Snow.

Victoria Archer (10)
Our Lady Of Ransom RC Primary School

Mac Rain

What trickles down your head and soaks your head?
It can make you soaking wet,
Who makes you take shelter down the lane?
Mac Rain.

What drips down the windowpane?
There it goes again
Dripping down the windowpane.
Mac Rain.

What bends the grass blades back?
It sometimes makes the sky turn black.
It makes the grass a silvery chain
Mac Rain.

The heavens break out,
It sounds as if someone's playing a drum
Rattling on the train
Mac Rain.

Callum Matthews (11)
Our Lady Of Ransom RC Primary School

Sam Sunshine

We can see him
We can't touch him
We can't hug him
We can't catch him on a line.
Sam Sunshine.

He gives us light
He makes things bright.
He gives us a tan,
He has plenty of time.
Sam Sunshine.

He stays at noon
He stays at eight pm.
He stays at six am.
He goes at night bye-bye
Sam Sunshine.

He's gone at night
He's gone at midnight
He's gone at late night
He comes at morning.
Sam Sunshine.

Michael Negus (11)
Our Lady Of Ransom RC Primary School

Friends

F riends are forgiving, friends don't forget
R eliable and trusting, you give them respect
I nteresting and great
E verlasting mates
N oisy and near, they comfort your fear
D angerous and daring
S omeone who is caring.

Matthew Netto (11)
Our Lady Of Ransom RC Primary School

World War II

The bravest men alive
With their family in their hearts as they strive
Into the battlefield they march
While bullets fly
And bombs hit the sky
And many die
So that others can live.

Myles Shaw (10)
Our Lady Of Ransom RC Primary School

Tam Hail

Who whistles at night
Waiting for someone to comfort him?
Who goes pale?
Tam Hail.

Who cries at night
Since he was guilty?
Who got bail?
Tam Hail.

Who gets up now and then
Always sad?
Who gets up to check the mail?
Tam Hail.

Who at night gets breeze?
Sometimes hot sometimes cold
From gale?
Tam Hail.

Hannah Rankin-Maclean (10)
Our Lady Of Ransom RC Primary School

Cron Hail

Who will make you
Turn pale?
Cron Hail.

When you take your dog for a walk
Who hits its tail?
Cron Hail.

Who hits your house hard
And destroys all your mail?
Cron Hail.

Who is fast and hard
And flows with the gale?
Cron Hail.

James Smith (10)
Our Lady Of Ransom RC Primary School

A Friendly Poem

F riends are together
R espect for each other
I   nclude your friends everywhere
E ven where you're not fair
N aughty friends are just right for me
D ifferences we cannot see
S mile every day with your friends.

Carmelina Di Lorenzo (11)
Our Lady Of Ransom RC Primary School

Spring Haiku

Golden sun dazzles
Running river flows gently
Fleecy white lambs bleat.

Rebecca Anastasi (11)
Our Lady Of Ransom RC Primary School

Snowy Day

Today is a snowy day
But you have to pay, so don't go out
Otherwise you have to delay.
Tomorrow is a snowy day
It's really cold but if you want to stay,
You don't have to pay.
Friday is a snowy day.
If you want to,
You can stay but get out of my way.
Saturday is not good, cos it didn't snow
But I wished it would,
I would play with the snow,
Snow hard and icy.

Richard Fernandes (11)
Our Lady Of Ransom RC Primary School

Still Snow

Who throws on the ground
as it burns into ice,
but when it's low?
Still Snow.

Who has their foe
as drops too low?
Still Snow.

Who has so much cold
as it bows down below?
Still Snow.

Joshua Wagstaff (10)
Our Lady Of Ransom RC Primary School

Mac Rain

What looks like bullets shooting from the sky?
Mac Rain.
What makes you tingle when it goes down your back?
Mac Rain.
What drops from the clouds up high?
Mac Rain.

What makes everything wet?
Mac Rain.
What makes big puddles?
Mac Rain.
What makes the snow not set?
Mac Rain.

Ryan Trevers (11)
Our Lady Of Ransom RC Primary School

The Alien

One day an alien came to Earth,
To see what he could see,
And when he came to visit me,
I made him a cup of tea.

I asked him if he could stay a while,
To show him round my house,
He said 'I'm in a hurry!'
I said, 'Please stay a while and have a curry!'

I asked him 'Where do you come from?'
He said 'I come from Mars'
I asked him, 'Where is that?'
He said, 'Up above the stars!'

Natalie East (11)
Our Lady Of Ransom RC Primary School

My Friendship Poem

Moving house is quite a scare
And I'll soon be going to a new school
I bet everyone will stare at me
And they'll all think I'm a fool.

I'm sitting on the bus
Waving my mum goodbye
What if they're not nice to me
And I just sit down and cry.

I'm looking at my school
It's my favourite colour green
It isn't like my old school
It's actually very clean.

I'm walking down the corridor
Looking at the colourful display
And all the models on the shelves
Are all made of clay.

My teacher welcomes me in
And her name is Miss Pegan
I'm sitting next to a really sweet girl
And she says her name is Megan.

Out in the cold and dark playground
Three girls did things in their own way
But leave me on the ice cold ground
Because coming this way is Miss Day.

Megan is coming over to me
A hand she has to lend
And all I have to say to her is
Thanks for being a true friend.

Catherine Hine (10)
Our Lady Of Ransom RC Primary School

The Friendship Alphabet

A ccept, they have a point of view
B ad times, we have a few of these
C aring, we should always be
D isapponted, we should make it up to them
E ager, to be friends with everyone
F riendly to you!
G ood times, these are treasured
H appy, this is the way I like to see you
I rritable, try not to be
J oke, make them laugh!
K eep, their secrets, Sshh!
L iar, this is not a true friend
M anage, to put up with different types of friends
N ever, break a promise
O nly, tell a secret if you believe in them
P al, a friend and comforter
Q uestion, you can ask them anything
R eliable and true but are you?
S pecial you are special because you are a friend
T oday, not just friends today or tomorrow but friends forever!
U nderstanding, to be this means a lot
V iew, see it from their point
W ait, they may not be true to you
X XX, you like to put this in a card to them
Y oung, or old, their friends it doesn't matter
Z est, friends have brought you this for life.

Elise Kemp (10)
Our Lady Of Ransom RC Primary School

Friendship Poem

F aithful to each other
R espect them like your brother
I nteresting is what a friend can be
E veryone with a friend is happy
N ew friends can be great
D on't forget your other mate
S orry is hard to say
H e or she will make up at the end of the day
I f they move away from each other
P ray that they will find another.

William Cooper (10)
Our Lady Of Ransom RC Primary School

Friendship

When I got into a squeak
I looked around, I took a peek.
At all the friends who were there for me
But one of my friends had told on me.
I went to the teacher I took the blame
And then I hung my head in shame
I asked my friends who told, I asked who
Do you think that friend was true?

Elizabeth Howell (10)
Our Lady Of Ransom RC Primary School

Rain Haiku

Rain is falling fast
The ice is freezing slowly
Soon the sun will come.

Liam Wheatley (10)
Our Lady Of Ransom RC Primary School

Snow

Some people say no to snow
But then again some people say hello
As it comes down low
It stops the river from its flow.

Who comes out?
Goes to your toes
As it blows
Some people moan.

As it very silently falls
I decorate house and road
Goes gold by the minute
I touch your hand.

What covers your car
And stops you from going far?
Is the snow
Really that bad?

Rebecca Smyth (10)
Our Lady Of Ransom RC Primary School

A Car

A steel hunk
A petrol drinker
A smooth runner
A regular hummer
A whiff of fame
A silky touch
A comfy traveller
A human server.

Jordan McKenna (11)
Our Lady Of Ransom RC Primary School

Midnight Fears

Twelve o'clock strikes
Twelve long beats
Of horror
The creaky door opens
Revealing the chains
Out come the phantoms and spirits
They creep up the stairs
And open my door
I tremble with fear
Then shriek out loud
The ghosts still come closer
And shake me quite hard
The clock then strikes 'One'
The ghosts hurry away
They hide in the clock
And never from then do
They haunt me.

Edward Hobbs (9)
Our Lady Of Ransom RC Primary School

Elephant!

A fat body,
A pancake-flat ear,
A smooth tusk,
A wrinkly trunk,
A stumpy foot,
A thin long tail,
A caring mother,
A storybook star!

Claire Petersen (11)
Our Lady Of Ransom RC Primary School

Under The Bed

There lives a monster under the bed,
I witnessed it creep up over my head.

It flew through the window wings outspread,
Its shiny scales were luminous red.

Two dark green eyes were looking at me,
They reminded me of the mossy cold sea.

Its jaws were open ready to eat,
Out of its mouth came unbearable heat.

It stared at me I gave it a grin
And scared, it soared straight into the bin.

The heat made me feel awkwardly funny,
When I woke up outside it was sunny.

Eleni-Maria Liaka (10)
Our Lady Of Ransom RC Primary School

The Goblins

T iny and troublesome
H ideous and hungry
E vil and envious

G rubby and grotty
O bviously ogre like
B utch and brainy
L urid and lazy
I cky and ice blooded
N oisy and naughty
S ly and sickly.

Rebecca Markham (11)
Our Lady Of Ransom RC Primary School

The Four Seasons

Spring brings a glorious feeling
As baby birds will soon chirp and sing,
Children start to play outside,
And days are getting warmer,
Trees start to blossom,
And then again it's summer.

Summer brings the joy of sun,
When people set their barbecues alight,
As kids are having loads of fun,
And teens have parties through the night,
Schools close for the summer holidays,
And cats lie around in the summer haze,
Then with a blink of an eye it's autumn.

Autumn is a lovely season,
When gardeners sow their seeds,
All the leaves turn brown and golden,
And the weather gives bulbs their needs,
Children go back to start a new school year,
And now frosty winter's getting near.

The most beautiful season is winter,
As the first snowflakes fall,
Children write their lists to Santa,
And stockings go up on the wall,
There are always Christmas cards to send,
Whilst people are getting colds and flu,
Now the seasons are coming to an end,
But don't worry, 'cause they'll be here again.

Rachel Jarrard (10)
Our Lady Of Ransom RC Primary School

The Mermaid's Lagoon

Who would be a mermaid fair, sitting alone combing her hair?
In the lagoon of singing choirs or was it just a bunch of liars
Who told me that there were mermaids in the lagoon?
A weep I heard was out of tune, from the mermaid in the lagoon,
Yes a mermaid was what I saw, now I know absolutely for sure
that there are mermaids in the lagoon.
I crept over to the sorrowful sound, then saw tears approach the
ground.
I asked what happened, what was done to the downcast lonely
one in the lagoon?
'I've lost my immense smile, for anywhere in the Nile, will bring
me no life but fill me with strife, like a nip of a crocodile' came
the reply from the mermaid in the lagoon.
'So train me to be talented in steps pace by pace, then I can show
them off tonight in the big mermaid race.'
'We will solve the current case,' I said to the mermaid in the lagoon.
She was a fast learner, but the race was about to start
I cheered her on with all my soul and heart.
Luckily she won and her joy was in me too.
'Thank you,' said the mermaid in the lagoon.
We had our separate ways to go, but now she's the mermaid
that I know.
I hope we meet again someday soon . . .

       Ssh top secret there are mermaids in the lagoon!

Kelsey Hibberd (9)
Our Lady Of Ransom RC Primary School

A Limerick

There was a young man called Ton,
Who loved playing badminton,
He played and played
Until the day did fade
That tired old man called Ton.

Georgia Colgate (11)
St John Fisher RC Primary School, Loughton

My Limerick

There was an old man from Epping
Who did a lot of stepping
He walked around
With his hound
That fit old man from Epping.

Thomas McLay (10)
St John Fisher RC Primary School, Loughton

Limerick

There was an old man from Spain
Who always loved to stand in the rain
He loved Spanish food
And he was very rude
That rude old man from Spain.

Annie Roberts (10)
St John Fisher RC Primary School, Loughton

Kennings

A beautiful feature
A lovely creature.

A fast runner
A high jumper.

A hay lover
A fur cover.

A lovely source
I am a horse.

Aoife Spillane (11)
St John Fisher RC Primary School, Loughton

Christmas Thank You

Dear Gran
Thanks for the shampoo
Can't wait till I grow hair
It was very thoughtful
I might use it on the wig
You got me last year.

Martin Woodhatch (11)
St John Fisher RC Primary School, Loughton

My Limerick

There was an old lady of Dingo
Who spent all her days at Bingo
She won ninety quid
Gave the rest to old Sid
That barmy old lady of Dingo.

Demi Jordan (10)
St John Fisher RC Primary School, Loughton

My Limerick

There was a young girl named Alice
Who lived in a rather strange palace
When she grew bigger
She worried about her figure
That rich young girl named Alice.

Alice Backham (10)
St John Fisher RC Primary School, Loughton

My Seven Wonders Of The World

Mount Everest is the cleverest
Of all murderers who make a kill
The grace and beauty leads all to believe
It's a wonderful place (with a trick up its sleeve).

The Northern Lights are a beautiful sight
That everyone should see
The elegance it shows makes people all around
Think themselves lucky for the free life they'd found.

The Niagara Falls have power to kill all
With thundering waves smashing the surface
The colossal fall from top to bottom
Makes a deafening roar, loud as thunder.

This offering from the French, America took, fists clenched
It is now America's prized possession
It's ever-going flame, never to be put out
It towers above all, it's beauty never in doubt.

Rainforests are dying, because of its murderers lying
It was known as the 'Garden of Eden'
The murderers are winning, because our minds aren't working
We are being vulnerable, so the killers are lurking.

If you see this sight, you will get a fright
Though it has no limit to beauty
This deadly thing has an unpredictable temper
So put on your helmets if you live anywhere near one.

This statue has gold, unknown, untold
And precious stones which no one knows.
It gives out beauty in rays of light
Only the sun could be more bright.

Adam Kelly (10)
St John Fisher RC Primary School, Loughton

Limericks

There was a young boy from Borridge
Who left home full of porridge.
One day by mistake,
He ate a large cake,
And exploded from here to Norwich.

Alice Knowles (10)
St John Fisher RC Primary School, Loughton

Snow

Snow, snow
It's so cool
Turn it into a snowball
Snow has come
The snow has gone
The snowman is just a con.

Christian Sweeting (10)
St John Fisher RC Primary School, Loughton

Guy Fawkes

The pathetic plot
The burning match.

The madman
The ultimate plan.

Caught in action
Guilty of treason.

Totally slaughtered
Hung, drawn and quartered.

Remember, remember
The fifth of November.

Jake Collier (10)
St John Fisher RC Primary School, Loughton

The Dentist

The dentist pushed my teeth out
and thought it was great fun.
He grabbed his pliers,
and dental priers
and pulled another one.

Yippee, hooray, what wonderful fun
he shouted out with glee.
He grinned a grin and went back in
and pulled out number three.

Then number four and number five
and number six and seven
were followed by a cheerful cry of
eight, nine, ten, eleven.

He took a few more from the top and
some from underneath.
He cranked them fat, until at last
he pulled out all my teeth.

Without my teeth I cannot chew
I just eat soup and mush
But don't be sad I'm kind of glad
I don't have to brush.

Tobi Adepoju (10)
St John Fisher RC Primary School, Loughton

Granny

Granny, Granny, in the street
Granny, Granny makes me smell her feet.
Try her dinner, she will not be a winner.
Granny, Granny is she dead or is she just asleep in bed?
Oops I think she fell on her head
As she got out of her bed.

Franchesca Sullivan (11)
St John Fisher RC Primary School, Loughton

Prose

1996 awesome, arachnid, fast and freaky.
Hidden a lot. Can't escape a rolled up paper.
Great acceleration,
Best in the nation, speedy kickster.
In exchange, its baby brother
In the pet shop.

1958 Boring aunt, angel cake.
Very classical. Absolutely
Hates *Kiss 100.*
Doesn't need fuel, needs clutch though.
Loves to chew on metal.
Will swap for a change of oil.

1987 Teenage sister, gone, you won't miss her.
Can't stop wheezing, but a hot tempered
PE coach settles that question.
Got no speed,
But comes with a free tyre pump.
In exchange a brother that's not so calm.

Antony Fray (10)
St John Fisher RC Primary School, Loughton

Christmas

Christmas comes once a year
When we think of loved ones dear.
Lighted trees all around,
Carols are the Christmas sound.

Children having lots of fun,
Opening presents one by one.
Sparkling eyes, smiling faces,
Around the world in different places.

People gather to share their joy,
For the birth of a special boy.
Jesus born in Bethlehem
Peace and happiness to all men.

Charlotte Fox (10)
St John Fisher RC Primary School, Loughton

Ocean

Oceans are the heart of the world,
the deep blue sea is one big treasure,
the waves are clashing claps.

The silence of the sea is breathtaking,
but the humming of the whales is peaceful,
the waves are smashing cymbals,
the dripping is like a triangle,
those are the instruments
of the ocean.

The motion of the ocean moves swiftly
with the reflection of the silver moon.
The time flies by, dawn has come,
the ocean awakes.

Margaret McGillicuddy (11)
St John Fisher RC Primary School, Loughton

Bonfires

A smell of smoke filling the air,
A sight of colourful light hitting the clear blue sky.

A sight of smiles on everybody's faces,
A feel of happiness.

A sudden sound of fireworks,
Hitting the air.

A peaceful sky
Filled with multicoloured sparkles.

A lighter zooming through the air
Fills the sky.

A warm blazing smoking smell
The 5th of November.

Alice Keenan (11)
St John Fisher RC Primary School, Loughton

Family Cars For Sale

1998 little sister, whinges like an old banger
Nothing a dummy wouldn't fix
Needs fuel but doesn't keep cool
Smaller model not available
Lasts for about a hundred years
In exchange for a quieter little sister.

1992 brother, fast but annoying
Quiet at times
Nothing a pinch wouldn't fix
Needs fizzy fuel to keep him cool
Larger model available but costs more
Will swap for a livelier brother.

1963 Mum, small but clever
Bossy at times
Nothing a relaxing sit down wouldn't fix
Colours may vary
Lasts for about fifty more years
Will not exchange for a taller Mum.

1958 Dad, old but efficient
A few grey hairs
Nothing a respray couldn't fix
Fixed model colours may vary
Will last for another forty five or more years
Will only swap for something quite unique.

1992 self, annoying but pretty
Talkative at times
Nothing a gag wouldn't fix
Runs on water
Hopes to live a good deal longer
Will swap for a jazzier model with sound system.

Caitriona Nolan (11)
St John Fisher RC Primary School, Loughton

Family And Friend Poem

1998 sister, as new as any other
Often makes runting noises
Failed MOT test
Does have a lot of exhaust
Slow model in exchange for quieter less broken sister
Runs on anything!

1992 sister very economical
Extremely noisy all the time
Needs gallons of fuel
Low mileage, no rust
Just gone to services
Will swap for something quite excellent.

1992 friend very sporty
Passed MOT only just
High mileage not much fuel or repairs
But has to go in for services
Runs on food and liquid
Will only swap for something quite unique.

Ruairidh Nolan (11)
St John Fisher RC Primary School, Loughton

Limericks

There was a young boy from Greece
Who had an outstanding big fleece
He went to the bakery
To buy some more pastries
That greedy young boy from Greece.

Kamile Ramanauskaite (11)
St John Fisher RC Primary School, Loughton

Spring

Spring, spring
Is so clean
Flowing through the trees
Sitting outside, in the yard
Watching the blossoms
Blooming fast.

Spring, spring
Is so clean
Flowing through the grass,
Bulbs start shooting through
Flowers start opening up.

Spring, spring
Is so clean
Flowing through the air
Birds start preparing their nests
Plants start budding from their shoots.

Chelsea Smith (10)
St John Fisher RC Primary School, Loughton

Magic Poems

There was an old witch who had a cat
And by the flick of her wand
The cat became a hat.

There was a wizard who got a shiver
And turned himself into slither
Then came the witch of Thane
And turned him back again.

There was a man who went to town
And thought his name was Jackie Chan.

Gemma Reilly (10)
St John Fisher RC Primary School, Loughton

Car Boot Sale

2002 Hamster. Fast and silent.
Needs waking up in the morning.
Uses up a bit of fuel.
Needs washing every day and cleaning out.
Very noisy at night.
In very good condition and doesn't need a lot of light.
Passed his MOT yesterday.
A very low mileage. 300 miles.
In exchange I'd like a slow fat hamster.

1999 Guinea Pig. Low mileage.
He's always awake and ready to go.
Makes a lot of noise and makes a very good burglar alarm.
Needs washing once a year and likes to stay outside
and run around.
Needs cleaning out once a week.
Doesn't use a lot of fuel up.
He sometimes needs a break.

9999999BC Granny.
Needs a few repairs on the wheels and engine.
Breaks down every day but can be fixed.
I am selling her at a good price for one dice.
Has met Jesus and got repaired.
Been to Heaven twice.
Is the oldest person alive!
Doesn't need cleaning, very quiet.
Her mileage is 1,000,000,000 miles.

Jack Gibson (11)
St John Fisher RC Primary School, Loughton

What If?

What if the world was square?
What if we didn't grow hair?

What if you could never die?
What if you could amazingly fly?

What if there was no money?
What if honey wasn't runny?

What if dogs learnt how to speak?
What if sweaty socks didn't reek?

What if teachers couldn't speak?
What if there was no week?

What if babies didn't drool?
What if there was no school?

What if there is no jail?
What if there was a holy grail?

What if there's no food that's nice
And all we ate was stir fried lice

What if, what if, what if?

Alec Vincent (10)
St John Fisher RC Primary School, Loughton

Thinking

Thinking is a part of me
It travels like a buzzing bee.

I don't know what I'd do without
I really wouldn't have a doubt.

I think about nearly everything,
Including, listening, talking and reading.

Thinking is important in my day
It's invisible, it's like an X-ray.

Jessica Porter (10)
St John Fisher RC Primary School, Loughton

Dolphin Poem

Dolphins are smooth
They glide and glide
Through the glistening waters.
They swim so silently
Tough and quick
Making a squeaky sound
Click-click-click.

They are friendly with humans.
They make fantastic shows.
They make people laugh
That's what I was told.
Shiny and soft that's what they are.
The grey and blue colour is right for them.
For dolphins are the best.

Hayley Donovan (11)
St John Fisher RC Primary School, Loughton

Mouse Stalker

A mouse stalker
A sleek walker.

A bird destroyer
A fish annoyer.

A quiet killer
A small tiddler.

I sit on the mat and of course
I'm a cat.

Stephen Rose (11)
St John Fisher RC Primary School, Loughton

Magical Best Friends

Harry Potter
Would never be a Trotter
He nearly died by Voldemort
I don't think Harry's got a single wart.

Hermione Granger
Wasn't born in a manger
She's a wonderful witch at Hogwarts
She can do spells of different sorts.

Ronald Weasley
Thinks everything's easy
He can't really do spells very well
He might as well give his wand to sell.

Nathalie Killoran (11)
St John Fisher RC Primary School, Loughton

My Cinquain

Wake up
Christmas is here
Frost all over the place
Downstairs presents are everywhere
Wicked.

Declan McGrenra (11)
St John Fisher RC Primary School, Loughton

Don't Do This, Don't Do That

Don't do this, don't do that,
Say it one more time, and I think I'll go mad!
Teachers telling me what to do,
I'm going to lose my mind and just get rude!
Mum and Dad always shouting at me,
Who could care less so just *leave me be!*

Ashley Rawlings (10)
St John Fisher RC Primary School, Loughton

The Moon

When it is dark, I become a white ball
Shining in the sky, like a crystal.
For when it is quiet, at the late hours of night,
I am the world's only light.
I can be strong, I can be dim,
Reflecting on water up to the brim.
I am always there, even if you can't see me
I am stuck in the sky and long to be free.

Nadia Parello (11)
St John Fisher RC Primary School, Loughton

Apples

A pples you are yummy I can see you all the time
P eople love to eat them not like lemon not like lime.
P eople pick apples all day long.
L isten to them singing the crunchy apple song.
E veryone eats apples, shiny red, or green,
S ort them out into groups and wash them till they're clean!

Ciaran Simpson (7)
St John Fisher RC Primary School, Loughton

Flowers

F lowers are red, flowers are blue, I wish I were a flower too.
L aughing in my yellow shoes.
O ver the hills living far away
W ait at the bus stop go out to play.
E ven flowers get energy
R unning around like a buzzy bee.
S o do you like flowers? Come on tell me!

Alexandra Bird (7)
St John Fisher RC Primary School, Loughton

School

S chool is great
C iaran's never late
H ush you've got to learn
O liver it's not your turn
O h no Miss Bloomfield's going to shout
L et's cover our ears without a doubt.

Lee Murray (7)
St John Fisher RC Primary School, Loughton

Apples

A n apple is so tasty and cold
P ick them up from the tree and let them be.
P eople will look at them and see how shiny they are.
L end them to the baker shop to buy at the bar.
E veryone will be as happy as can be,
S ee the apples grow on every apple tree.

Andrew Stevens (7)
St John Fisher RC Primary School, Loughton

The Young Girl Of Steed

There was a young girl of Steed
Who had always loved to read
She sat there all day
Just reading away
That young bookworm of Steed.

Leah Sullivan (10)
St John Fisher RC Primary School, Loughton

War

The colour of war is grey
War smells like sulphur
It tastes like steel
War sounds like cannons being fired
War lives in Hell!

Adam Gordon (9)
St John Fisher RC Primary School, Loughton

War

War is red,
It smells like fire,
It tastes like black blood
It sounds like people screaming together
It feels like death
And lives in a volcano.

Maria Spillane (9)
St John Fisher RC Primary School, Loughton

Anger

Anger is red like blood
It smells like tar and diesel petrol,
It tastes soggy, sour and rotten,
It sounds like chalk screeching against a blackboard,
Anger feels sharp, rough and slimy,
It lives in the bottom of your heart.

Conor O'Rourke (9)
St John Fisher RC Primary School, Loughton

Love

Love feels like a big fluffy cushion
with butterflies flying around you.
Love tastes like a big cake with
candles and lights.
Love smells like a bottle of rose perfume
and delights.
Love sounds like the gentle sea and
romantic music.

Caitlin Salter (9)
St John Fisher RC Primary School, Loughton

Anger

Anger is red
Anger smells like smoke
Anger tastes like chilli
Anger sounds like a plane landing
Anger feels painful
Anger lives in the century.

Rebecca Trusson (9)
St John Fisher RC Primary School, Loughton

Fear

Fear is like a bolt of lightning
It is scary, fierce and frightening.
It feels like you are not there,
It lives in your heart, body and everywhere.
It also feels like you are weak on the floor.
It looks like a silver dash,
It flows through your veins in a flash.

Max Wells (9)
St John Fisher RC Primary School, Loughton

Happiness

It is like a yellow light for joy and love
It is like the smell of sweet flowers on a summer's day
It is like the taste of sugary sweet things
It is like the sound of laughter, *hip hip hooray*
It is like the feeling of fun and joy because that's its meaning
And it lives in the hearts of people where happiness will remain
       For ever.

Amy Marsh (9)
St John Fisher RC Primary School, Loughton

Sadness

Sadness is horrible
It can also make you feel bad or sick.
Sadness is a kind of hurting pain
So cry it out before it hurts you.

Elena Guthrie (9)
St John Fisher RC Primary School, Loughton

War

War is black and it leaves tracks
It smells like smoke
And it tastes like food that makes you choke
It sounds like a bomb exploding
It feels like a rock that cannot be broken
It lives in the main part of an earthquake.

Martin Laffey (10)
St John Fisher RC Primary School, Loughton

War!

War is cruel
Its colour is black
Its smell is dirty air
It tastes like pain
It sounds like screams
It feels scary
It lives in the bottom of your heart.

Danny Gough (9)
St John Fisher RC Primary School, Loughton

War!

Its colour is darkened grey
It smells like tortured blood
It tastes like rotten rats
It sounds bitter
It feels like fire
It lives in the world.

Amy Wallace (9)
St John Fisher RC Primary School, Loughton

Death

Death is black
It smells like dirty blood
Death tastes like mouldy eggs
It sounds like lightning
Death feels like damp grass
It lives in a graveyard.

Kiera McEvoy (9)
St John Fisher RC Primary School, Loughton

Anger

Anger is black
   Anger smells like smoke
      Anger tastes like blood
         Anger sounds like wind
            Anger feels like a sharp, hard rock.
               It lives in a dark and gloomy cave.

Alice Slisz (9)
St John Fisher RC Primary School, Loughton

Love

Love is pink.
It smells like roses blooming on
A beautiful spring day.
It tastes like strawberries,
Sugar and cream.
It feels soft and silky,
And it lives inside your own
Heart.

Rachael Keeling (9)
St John Fisher RC Primary School, Loughton

Love

The colour pink
It smells of blossoming flowers
It tastes like strawberries and sugar
It sounds like an angel playing a harp
It feels soft and fluffy
It lives in people's hearts.

Gabriella Difrancesco (9)
St John Fisher RC Primary School, Loughton

Who Am I?

I jump deep blue waves,
Explore dark murky caves,
Swim with the beautiful mermaids,
That sing on my sad blue days,
Swiftly swim through coral reef,
Gobbling up tiny fish to make strong teeth,
I see different things every way,
And I go further every day.
I see, swim, leap in,
I splash, bash, dash and smash,
I jump the waves in glee,
I will show you what life can be.

Natalie Campling (10)
St John Fisher RC Primary School, Loughton

Barn Owl

Forest walker
Great stalker
Big and white
Hunts at night
Extremely silent
Never violent
Great big eyes
Also flies
Hunts and kills
Shrieks and thrills
Lives in a barn
Means no harm.

James Cambridge (11)
St Michael's Preparatory School, Leigh-on-Sea

My Cat Needs

He needs:

Fur that shines like the golden sun in the sky
Eyes that glisten like a box of diamonds
Personality that is like a young child
The adventurousness that lasts forever like the love
in a heart
The sweet face like a baby smiling for the first time
Skill like a wild panther balancing on branches.

Leanne Saunders (11)
St Michael's Preparatory School, Leigh-on-Sea

My Dog Needs

He needs:

A nose that smells like a hungry lion,
Paws that pad like a person stamping
A bark that echoes like a cry in the night

Bravery of a knight in armour
Acceleration of a speeding car
Soul of a good samaritan.

Jack Byrne (11)
St Michael's Preparatory School, Leigh-on-Sea

A Cat's Life

He needs
Fur that protects like a woolly coat in winter
Claws that cut like a hot knife through butter
Eyes that glow like a candle in the dark
Curiosity like a fox round a bin
Purr that rumbles like distant thunder
Energy of a child who's had too much sugar
Agility of a wild deer speeding away from a predator.

Alex Nagle (10)
St Michael's Preparatory School, Leigh-on-Sea

My Cat

Sharp claws
Jagged jaws

Gleaming eyes
Soft paws

Always tries
Never lies

Long tail
Very pale

Plays ball
Always crawls

Very clever
Stays forever.

Hannan Imran (11)
St Michael's Preparatory School, Leigh-on-Sea

What My Cat Has

Furry paws
Tiny jaws
Always stalks
Never talks
Warm home
Never moan
Large nose
Tiny toes
Big belly
Like jelly
Long tail
Never flails.

Scott Bunting (11)
St Michael's Preparatory School, Leigh-on-Sea

A Tiger

He needs,
A tail that twitches like trees in a storm
Eyes that glow like stars in the night
Fur that shivers like a bitterly cold morning.

The bravery of a soldier in a battle
The energy of a cheetah catching his prey
The courage of a firefighter that's saving someone.

Amit Lal (11)
St Michael's Preparatory School, Leigh-on-Sea

Big Bear

It needs:

Fur that's warm like a fire in the wood,
Eyes that glow like nuclear power,
A roar that rumbles like thunder in the night.

Bravery like a knight in battle,
Skill like a footballer,
Energy like an athlete.

Henry Howard (11)
St Michael's Preparatory School, Leigh-on-Sea

To Dress A Haggis

To dress up a haggis smart as can be,
First ask the haggis what it wants to be,
If it says a builder, dress it up in red,
And give it mini tools in a mini garden shed.
If it says a waiter dress it up in black,
Then all you need to do is provide a small top hat.

Felicity Dicks (11)
St Michael's Preparatory School, Leigh-on-Sea

The Mountain Deer

He needs,
Ears that point like the head of an arrow,
A body that leaps like a coiled spring,
Legs that are more elegant like a diamond chandelier,
Steadiness of a lighthouse in the wind,
Agility of Spiderman on a web,
Attentiveness of a curious schoolboy.

Billy Lake (10)
St Michael's Preparatory School, Leigh-on-Sea

My Dog Needs

She needs
A wet nose that glistens in the sun like ripples of water
A tail that thumps like the beat of a drum
Paws that pad like bears wandering around.

Mischief of a little toddler
Naughtiness of a cheeky monkey
Adventurous as a greedy wolf.

Danielle Austin (11)
St Michael's Preparatory School, Leigh-on-Sea

The Grizzly Bear

A body as big as a bus
Eyes that glow like a candle in the dark
Fur as tough as a rope
Claws that scrape like a chisel
Bravery as to be a saviour for others
Ferocity like a soldier in a war
The agility of a galloping horse.

Jack Booth (11)
St Michael's Preparatory School, Leigh-on-Sea

Lion

He needs
Eyes that shine like a devil in a cave
Fur that is smooth like a baby's bottom
A roar that blows like a blizzard of snow

Skill that kills like a fox hunter
Energy that powers like a rocket
Personality that shows like a celebrity.

Luke Snoad (11)
St Michael's Preparatory School, Leigh-on-Sea

The Dragon

Fire breath
Causes death
Green scales
Feasts on males
Red spikes
Eats Mikes
Sharp teeth
Spiky leaf.

Emily Ackers (10)
St Michael's Preparatory School, Leigh-on-Sea

Eagle Eyes

Wings that glide like a leaf in the wind
Eyes that glow like stars in the night
Claws that pierce like a hot knife in butter
Courage of a knight in shining armour
A cry that pierces the heart like a gun
Discipline like a soldier marching to war
Dignity like a dying man in battle
Heart of a saviour helping the public.

Shashank Sivaji (11)
St Michael's Preparatory School, Leigh-on-Sea

The Lion

Fearsome jaws
Furry paws

Large giant
Sometimes silent

Hungry beast
Meat feast

Non talker
Jungle walker

Thick hair
Never cares

Warm home
Never moans

Sharp ears
Hates spears.

Tom Martin (10)
St Michael's Preparatory School, Leigh-on-Sea

My Family

My family is crazy you wouldn't believe it,
My big brother Roger's a bit of a nitwit.

Great Uncle Pete has stinky feet
But Auntie Jane oh isn't she sweet.

My mum Mary-Kate drives like a looney,
My dad called Fred thinks he's Wayne Rooney.

Grandad Dave has a head like an egg,
Nana Susan has an old wooden leg.

So now you have seen my family tree
But wait I haven't mentioned me.

Leanne Coutts (10)
St Michael's Preparatory School, Leigh-on-Sea

Mittens On Kittens

Candy and Flossy are two little kittens,
Eight tiny paws like snow white mittens.

They play like children hour after hour,
In comes Mum and they start to cower.

Their noses so wet so squidgy so cute,
Walking along with their paws on mute.

Licking and purring like their mum,
Waiting for me to tickle their tum.

Eyes that glint like a candle at night,
Looking so innocent they start up a fight.

Two tails that flick over again,
A purr that sounds like a motor on a train.

Once the time's gone for them to be fed,
Up the stairs and off to bed.

Gemma Willis (10)
St Michael's Preparatory School, Leigh-on-Sea

My Kittens

Spike the kitten is a little tyke,
Jumps like a tiger on his brother Mike.

His brother Mike is such a timid fellow,
With his eyes like street lamps green and yellow.

They light up dark and stormy nights,
Even when he's in the worst cat fight.

They always play on our old couch,
After having a juicy Whiskas pouch.

Spike's eyes are as amber as can be,
He takes away all my anger by looking at me.

Georgie Hunt (11)
St Michael's Preparatory School, Leigh-on-Sea

Pat The Cat

Pat the cat has paws of silk
Eyes as white as creamy milk.

His tail a wonderful summer night
With a soft touch mysterious light.

His purr is a motor, sweet and soft
His ears as velvety as a cloth.

Pat has a nose wet and sleek
His teeth as strong as a beak.

His smile is charming and kind
His body elegant fine.

Pat has a soggy wet tongue
Which pumps up and down like a lung.

He is such a good friend to me
He makes me happy as can be.

Abeera Imran (10)
St Michael's Preparatory School, Leigh-on-Sea

Rosey The Puppy

Rosey the puppy has ears like silk,
She's always lapping creamy milk.

Her coat so smooth and very sleek,
Shiny and glossy week after week.

Her nose so rubbery like a ball,
Her paws so wet, rough and small.

Her tail wags from side to side,
As her legs are skidding wide.

Her panting reminds me of a steam train,
As she plods along in gentle rain.

Caroline Terry (11)
St Michael's Preparatory School, Leigh-on-Sea

Peace

Peace is the stillness
Like silence in a room.

White gives a quietness
When there is no gloom.

Scented candles that flicker
And make you feel calm.

Like the light in your heart
From the friend with the charm.

A smile is a companion
When you're feeling sad.

Which makes the peace
When you're feeling mad.

So that's what brings
The peace in our lives.

When peace is not there
My heart strives.

Poppy Etheridge (11)
St Michael's Preparatory School, Leigh-on-Sea

Happy Hamster

He needs
Eyes that stare at you like a sad person
Teeth that twinkle like a razor blade
Pouches that fill with food like a hot air balloon
A nose that's the colour like a little pink button
Paws that are small like soft little sponges
Belly that's squashy like wobbly jelly
Fur that's soft and warm like velvet and silk.

James Husselbee (10)
St Michael's Preparatory School, Leigh-on-Sea

Friendship

Friends are someone you can trust,
People that are faithful.

They'll be there both today and tomorrow,
Friends stand by you in your sorrow.

They stand by you in thick and thin,
Doesn't matter if you lose or win.

They help you when you're sad and lonely,
A friend is a companion the one and only.

No worries what their name might be,
Whether it's George, Emma or even Harry.

They will be there in good or bad,
True friends are there when you are sad.

Emily Lodge (11)
St Michael's Preparatory School, Leigh-on-Sea

Forever Friends

Friends are a comfort,
Like a hug from your mum.

Friends give you happiness,
Joy, laughter and fun.

Friends give you encouragement,
Which fills you with hope.

Friends are the aid,
Which help you to cope.

Friends make you happy,
They make you feel glad.

Friends are there to reassure you,
When you are feeling sad.

Hannah Webster (10)
St Michael's Preparatory School, Leigh-on-Sea

Feline Facts

Treasure the cat has a purr like a motor
Echoing the house it can be quite a bother.

His tail gives a thump that vibrates through the house,
But being so loving he would not hurt a mouse.

His silky fur is the vision of golden thread,
And appears as a sunbeam at the end of the bed.

His ears stick up like the point of a blade,
And returns to the garden, his mountainous glade.

His eyes give a glisten, like that of a crystal,
And his teeth are as sharp as a wild green thistle.

Claire Towler (10)
St Michael's Preparatory School, Leigh-on-Sea

Perfect Pupil

He/She needs:
A brain that whizzes like a roller coaster ride,
A head with intelligence that needs no sort of guide.
Eyes that watch like a hawk out hunting,
Innocence to beat even Baby Bunting.
Ears that absorb sounds like bats searching for prey,
An interest in subjects that is used all day.
Legs that run in the Sports Day races,
Fingers to constantly do up laces.
Hands that write like JK Rowling,
A good excuse when caught out prowling!

Ashton Moore   (11)
St Michael's Preparatory School, Leigh-on-Sea

Jimbob The Farmer

Jimbob the farmer has a hat like a cat,
And a jacket that's older than a 1960's flat.

His house is a caravan it was in Devon,
Until, it got towed down the A127.

His wife is called Sandra she is so weird
She's got a head like a pumpkin and a ten foot long beard.

His son Davey Crocket who is only three thinks he's an elf,
Because he was born up a tree.

His aunt was called Florence and was such a nuisance
He pushed her down the stairs just for the insurance.

Owen Lucas (10)
St Michael's Preparatory School, Leigh-on-Sea

Arnie

Arnie the dog has to bite
With a milky stalactite.

He wheezes and sneezes in the rain
Every time yelping in pain.

He was never a good sailor
But has a first-class tailor.

His tail a brown and black rota
Always a working non-stop motor.

He likes the cat
And sees like a bat.

Mateo Dworkin (10)
St Michael's Preparatory School, Leigh-on-Sea

Dreaming The Cyclops

I dreamed I saw a Cyclops with
Only one eye
I dreamed that it would go away
Or maybe even die
By good giants or by ogres.

But then before I yell
'Help me friends'
He tells me it's
Not the end
Because he is my friend.

Now you are coming
With me
All the time
You will be free
To wander with me.

He would take me really high
Into the night sky
Why does he not talk to me?
I really want to fly
Into the night sky.

Aarib Rajulawalla (8)
St Michael's Preparatory School, Leigh-on-Sea

Perfect Pet

She needs
A name that is known through the street.
The lovely soft sound from her cute little feet.
The eyes of green and blue the same.
As you should know these pets are tamed.
Ears that are soft and gentle at touch.
If you have one you should love it very much.

Molly Jupitus (10)
St Michael's Preparatory School, Leigh-on-Sea

Poppy The Kitten

Poppy the kitten has whiskers like thread
A little pink nose and lap for a bed.

Her purr's like the engine of a rumbling car
And when she goes wondering she never goes far.

When it's time to be fed she trots into the room
And hopes for a stroke and a soft gentle groom.

Around her ankles her fur is shiny white
Like snow that's fallen in the dark of the night.

Laura Stennett (11)
St Michael's Preparatory School, Leigh-on-Sea

The Dragon's Castle

It was quiet, I sensed the dragon
The pathway jagged and round
The huge gates to the castle.

It is still, I sense the dragon
The gate towers above me
The bolts stare boldly.

It is dusk, I sense the dragon
The doors open inwardly
The stone floor glaring.

It is dark, I sense the dragon
Step by step each foot walks
Forward carefully
One by one.

It is quiet, I sense the dragon
Eyes looking side by side
A flash ahead.

It is still, I sense the dragon
The dragon is here right now
Now where is it
I sense the dragon . . .

Michael Kamdar (8)
St Michael's Preparatory School, Leigh-on-Sea

A Monster In My Wardrobe

When I get into bed
I see my wardrobe clearly in sight,
Look at it what I see
A claw straightening up just to catch me!

Listen I tell you it's a monster I see
Just wait till it tries to catch me
Oh dear it's coming out
What shall I do?

It's creeping up on me
At least my light is still on
But I think he's going to
Turn out my light.

There's nothing more that I don't like
Than being left alone on a dark night
In my room I am scared to death
Phew it's only Dad, cos I should be asleep.

Timothy Berry (8)
St Michael's Preparatory School, Leigh-on-Sea

The Seagull

The seagull flies through the air
Taking very good care
He's looking for something to eat
Just as a man sat on a seat.

He then spies a fly
But he doesn't know that he's going to die
He just took off from a bin
The seagull thinks he's going to sigh.

Soon the fly goes into a house
It buzzes past a sleeping mouse
Near the greenhouse
Along comes the seagull and catches the fly
Now the fly has to die.

Jack Abbott (9)
St Michael's Preparatory School, Leigh-on-Sea

Tick-Tock Clock

The tick-tock clock ticked and tocked every day, every while,
You can hear it for a mile,
You go to a shop you can hear it well when you go to buy a bell.

Blue or yellow, green and pink,
These are the colours which give you the pedallant clink,
She ticked and tocked the little clock meant she liked the
feel of felt.

The little clock ticked for me to see,
But yet she did not answer me,
She hated me,
That's what I felt,
I thought my heart had to melt.

Oriana Nerberka (9)
St Michael's Preparatory School, Leigh-on-Sea

Coke

My mum says
Don't drink too much Coke
Or your teeth will dissolve and you will choke.

My mum says
Don't drink too much Coke
Or you'll have to have fillings
And they cost many shillings.

My mum says
There are too many chemicals in Coke
That can give you a stroke.

But . . . I say
I love the bubbles in my throat
Making my head feel afloat
Now they even have vanilla Coke
Which is a favourite of some folk.

Parum Cheema (8)
St Michael's Preparatory School, Leigh-on-Sea

Dreaming The Phoenix

I dreamed I saw a Phoenix
Gliding in the forest sky
Gracefully flying to her tree
And out of her beak came a long, deep sigh.

Then I realised that she was pregnant
I also saw that she was hurt
For on her leg was a deep, deep cut
For a bandage I tore a piece of my shirt.

Then she knew what I had done
And gratefully let me watch under the sun
I found out that the Phoenix could talk
Her name was Tally and she was great fun.

Tally had names for her three
Kelly, Carly and Emily.
I thought they were pretty all those names
And just then there was a bunch of red and orange flames.

Tally told me this was a sign
Telling her the chicks were near
I lifted my ear to Tally's tummy
And a little peep, peep I could hear.

When I woke up in my bed
I had a throbbing in my head
But beside my bed in a purple jar
Were six golden egg shells from afar.

Sasha Dworkin (9)
St Michael's Preparatory School, Leigh-on-Sea

Dreaming Of Fairies

I dreamt I saw a fairy,
Last night . . .
Tiptoeing across the grass
Her wings shining bright . . .

I saw her in the grass,
I saw the grass pass . . .
In the wind,
The branches rustled in their sleep
A fairy wept . . .

I saw a fairy dancing in the moonlight,
Her wings glittering all night . . .
Dancing on the water, it was such a sight
Under the shining stars so bright . . .

Then I saw the Queen,
The fairies were all clean . . .
I watched this all night,
The fairies dancing in the light . . .

The fairies left me something,
It was golden dust!
The fairies told me to use it on things that rust . . .
I never saw the fairies again,
But the dust worked all the same.

Alexandra Morgan (8)
St Michael's Preparatory School, Leigh-on-Sea

The Talk Of The Sea

The sea, so blue and white
Like dreamy cream being poured into life.
The waves like little, pink horses, as they
gush to the ends of the beach
in the light of hazel, coloured sunbeams . . .

The wind streaming through the air,
the seagulls gently singing a tune.
The sea, being touched by a flicker of rain,
which dropped with a grey, misty cloud . . .

The sea, so deep and clear,
like water in a glass of blue dye.
So still, calm, silent and peaceful,
that you can hear the splash of the mermaids
tail . .

The sun, as a horizon in a paradise land
Making the sky change colour at night.
The sun, down on the sea,
Turning it red and orange . . .

How wonderful it looks, as you stare into the sky,
But now, the sea, all grey, slow, dense and thick,
The world as black as charcoal and blackhole . . .

Polluting the nature of its colours,
Letting creatures die, at its fault
As we waste all its beauty and life,
through giving it food as our throw aways.
The sea couldn't be more dull
than it is, right now.

Tyra Packer (9)
St Michael's Preparatory School, Leigh-on-Sea

The Playground

The playground is the place to be
Just listen closely and you'll see
For when the bell rings out for break
My friends and I we start to shake.

There's football, netball even chess
But basketball I love the best
You sometimes see me slip and fall
Or bang my head against the wall.

We are often playing games like 'It'
It's lots of fun and keeps us fit
The teachers watch and keep an eye
In case any children start to cry.

I hope I never get detention
Because missing break will give me tension
Now when the bell goes we are done
But we can say we had great fun.

Harrison Payne (9)
St Michael's Preparatory School, Leigh-on-Sea

Mind Readers

Animal aquarium
Tiger tail
Violet pilot
Snowy Chloe
Luscious lolly
Jolly Polly

Headache

Horrible history
Spider spooky
Red head
Nutty nooty
Sooty looty.

Amreen Rajulawalla (10)
St Michael's Preparatory School, Leigh-on-Sea

Dreaming Of Pegasus

I dreamed I saw a flying horse,
He flew through a starry night.
He was Pegasus by name, of course,
He dived and twirled and smiled at me.

He was a legend of white feathers.
He flew around and around my house.
His mane was a stream of white heathers.
He swooped past my window,
His wings beating mightily.

He was pearly white,
He glistened through a carpet of black.
He was gliding in a moonlight flight.
I longed to go and fly with him.

A gush of wind whirled around my head.
I was cold and tried to touch my dream,
But I woke up, back in my bed.
There resting on my palm
Was a hair, like a wave from a snow white
Stream.

Rosie Shead (9)
St Michael's Preparatory School, Leigh-on-Sea

My Creation Of The World

It needs:

Brightness like a bunch of flowers,
which are tall and slender like elegant towers.

Heat that bakes like a hot farrier's fire,
shining in the darkness like polished wire.

Water that is refreshing like a new year at school
making lagoons, rivers and sometimes a pool.

Undulating land like a carved piece of wood,
providing shelter and homes for everything good.

Sarah Pryor (11)
St Michael's Preparatory School, Leigh-on-Sea

Dreaming The Dragon

I thought I saw a dragon last night
It stomped through the forest,
Almost out of sight,
Sniffling a starlight silence.

Its single tail
Stood waving like a lance,
I saw him shake his bald head
And snuffle and glance
And paw the silent air.
His fire was like a mass of red hair.

My brain was mad, and not clear.
I could hardly think or speak.
Above my mind, I heard the ground creak
And then, where I stood,
I heard it stomp off into the wood,
Into the dark space between the trees.

A sudden rush of a rapid night breeze,
That felt both cold and deep,
Woke me from my night sleep,
And there on my pillow beside my head
Was a piece of golden red thread.

I still have that piece of mane,
I keep it still,
Inside a vase on my window sill
And Britain hangs heavy
On my brain,
It helps me think of the dragon again.

Jonathan Kerridge (9)
St Michael's Preparatory School, Leigh-on-Sea

The Dream Dragon

As I lie in my bed
I see a dragon in my head
He has amber eyes
And a spiky tail
And he is drinking lots of ale!
I can't believe what I see
Then he stops and turns to me
I was wrong about the dragon
I see he has a friendly face
Even his scales look like lace
I talk to him and say
What's your name anyway?
He doesn't reply, I don't know why
Then I see
The dragon is fading silently
Then he says to me
I have been a long time dead
Because I live in your head.

Charlotte Allum (9)
St Michael's Preparatory School, Leigh-on-Sea

Courageous Features

A rabbit needs,
Eyes that glimmer like the sun on a hot summer's day,
Paws that slice like a blade cutting through meat,
Ears that shiver like a hand on a frigid winter's night,
A nose that jolts like thunder descending,
A tail that twitches like rustling of leaves,
A courage that never gives up like a spiritual warrior.

Alex Tharmaratnam (10)
St Michael's Preparatory School, Leigh-on-Sea

Teacher's Revenge?

'Let's get them back,' said Mr Crane
'They stole my pencil case again.'
'Those wicked kids!' screamed Mrs Spike
'They stole my brand new mountain bike.'
'I understand,' croaked Mr Pot
'They made my tea get scorching hot.'

Above all this Miss Zevenge did say
'We'll give them our teacher's revenge today.'

But standing by the staffroom door was a little girl called Eleanor,
She ran and told old Mrs Broom who worked inside the science room.
Now Mrs Broom wore a pointy black hat and on her desk lay a
crafty black cat.
Upon a little stool she sat brewing a potion or something like that.
Eleanor ran in and said, 'They're making such an awful fuss
And plotting to make fun of us.'
Mrs Broom just smiled and said, 'I read the thoughts inside your head
Now you go back to class with glee and leave the rest to little old me.'

'Right 4L, a test we'll do, get down to it without further ado.'
A flash, a bang, the teacher screamed, fell on the floor
Then slid out the classroom door.
The children sat in great dismay their classroom all in disarray.
But soon there came a great big cheer, for their new teacher
did appear.
Hurrah, hurrah, for Mrs Broom who *used* to work in the science room.

Edina Fisher-Allen (9)
St Michael's Preparatory School, Leigh-on-Sea

The Dream Of The Fairy

I dreamed I saw the fairy late last night
She twinkled through the moonlight dropping sparkle in the light
Looking down at me.

Her pink wings
Flattered like a butterfly
I saw her silver crown and the twinkle in her eye
And she matches the midnight air,
Her dress like a mass of golden hair.

My head was spinning round
I nearly touched the ground
Above me I heard the fairy.

In my bed I silently lay
Then I heard my mother say
'Darling, it's time to get up.'

Georgia Gibbins (9)
St Michael's Preparatory School, Leigh-on-Sea

My Extraordinary Mind

Strawberry stars
Rabbit running
Purple circle
Sunny funny
Stringy spaghetti
Betty settee.

Headache

Ghastly gore
Creepy cockroach
Green bean
Rainy daily
Awful asparagus
Bus suss.

Samantha Fletcher   (10)
St Michael's Preparatory School, Leigh-on-Sea

Mind Words

Freddy frog
Froggy fishing
Pink wink
Sunny funny
Saucy spaghetti
Yeti Betty.

Headache

Hell headache
Spider spinning
Gory grey
Wet winter
Creepy cucumber
Sleeping slumber.

Olivia Clark (10)
St Michael's Preparatory School, Leigh-on-Sea

My Mind

Kangaroo Karl
Dog doomed
Red said
Snow bow
Perfect pasta
Addictive Casper.

Headache

Vomiting verbal reasoning
Porcupine parrots
Cauliflower every hour
Rain pain
Pale yellow
Bail bellow.

Karl Anderson (9)
St Michael's Preparatory School, Leigh-on-Sea

Brain Confusing

Kangaroo key
Dicraeosaurus doom dead
Turquoise boys
Hurricane train
Spaghetti spicy
Sizzling nicely.

Headache

Awful Arsenal
Crinkly crab
Rotten red
Frowning fog
Cabbage crawling
All appalling.

Christopher Drube (10)
St Michael's Preparatory School, Leigh-on-Sea

Super Duper Mind

Chelsea cheering
Chinchilla choking
Violet pilot
Sunny honey
Spaghetti squiggling
Wriggling sizzling.

Headache

Evil Arsenal
Creepy cockroach
Pink stink
Rainy painy
Rotten fish
On a dish.

Ronnie Winmill (9)
St Michael's Preparatory School, Leigh-on-Sea

The Supernatural Mind

Zoro zoo
Penguin pie
Blue moo
Freezing teasing
Chunky chips
Licking lips.

Headache

Chelsea cowards
Killing cats
Pink stink
Misty wristy
Vomiting vegetables
Writing illegible.

James Grant (10)
St Michael's Preparatory School, Leigh-on-Sea

Mind Words

Television tots
Cat curl
Blue clue
Sunny bunny
Spaghetti springy
Everyone bringy.

Headache

Yellow yak
Rat rap
Orange lozenge
Foggy hoggy
Lonesome leek
Hide-and-seek.

Katharine East (9)
St Michael's Preparatory School, Leigh-on-Sea

Mind Readers

Sock sauce
Lima lollies
Dark green
Uno extreme
Rain pain
Mucky mash
Lovely eyelash
Go in a dash
Lots of cash
Sticky grey tash.

Headache

Ghastly geography
Sickly scorpion
Stinky pinkie
Hail rail
Fungus fish
Rubbish wish
Mum's mean dish.

Hannah Stennett (9)
St Michael's Preparatory School, Leigh-on-Sea

What A Dog Needs

He needs
A tail that sways like a leaf in the breeze,
A nose as wet as a soggy ball,
A bark as sharp as the blade of a knife,
Fur as soft as a piece of silk,
A heart to care for other people,
Love for nature all around.

William Todd (10)
St Michael's Preparatory School, Leigh-on-Sea

Mind Reader

Saucy sea
Bunny bun
Blue glue
Snowy blowy
Crunchy chips
Munchy dips.

Headache

Manchester United
Muck
Scrawny sharks
Stinky pinky
Duck unluck
Bashy mashy
Dashy clashy.

Alice Stone (9)
St Michael's Preparatory School, Leigh-on-Sea

Mind Words

Apple Alex
Doggy joggy
Green mean
Sunny money
Chunky chips
Licking lips.

Headache

Freaky fire
Silly snake
Pink stink
Icy micey
Big beans
Very mean.

Alex Capewell (9)
St Michael's Preparatory School, Leigh-on-Sea

Mind Words

Top Ten
Tiger teeth
Blue glue
Snowy blowy
Crusty cake
That I bake.

Headache

Enormous elephants
Spider scary
Black bat
Rain pain
Bad baked beans
Big mean greens.

Jessica Tan   (10)
St Michael's Preparatory School, Leigh-on-Sea

Supernatural Mind

Wobbly what
Squirrel's swamp
Lemon demon
Rain pain
Nourishing spinach
Greenwich pilgrimage.

Headache

Hurry hunt
Mongoose mucky
Sapphire classify
Ice spice
Quiche teach
Peach bleach.

Peter Waterman   (9)
St Michael's Preparatory School, Leigh-on-Sea

The Brain's Brandy

Koala kick
Budgie badger
Silver Wilbur
Sandy storm warm
Lovely laces
Braces faces.

Headache

Yellow yak
Hedgehog hair
Black tack
Gloom doom
Sickly stew
Glue boo.

Jack Benn-Woolley (9)
St Michael's Preparatory School, Leigh-on-Sea

Mind Words

Gummy gums
Alligator terminator
Yellow fellow
Windy Cindy
Fake steak
Tummyache

Headache

Cruel Arsenal
Hairy hedgehog
Pink stink
Sunny bunny
Bibs ribs
Fibs cribs.

George Goldring (10)
St Michael's Preparatory School, Leigh-on-Sea

Mind Reading

Didi daydream
Doggy doodle
Blue clue
Snowy blowy
Spaghetti scrummy
Yummy tummy.

Headache

Gladiator gory
Spider cider
Red bled
Rainy painy
Floppy fish
Missed kiss.

Deanna Jacques (10)
St Michael's Preparatory School, Leigh-on-Sea

Mind Readers

Flossy flea
Doggy doodles
Blue clue
Sunny bunny
Cadbury chocolate
Pleasing plate.

Headache

X-ray xylophone
Ratty rats
Black crack
Icy micy
Terror tomatoes
Frozen toes.

Bethany Dunn (9)
St Michael's Preparatory School, Leigh-on-Sea

Headache

Tacky turban
Spooky spider
Down with brown
Brainy rainy
Bossy butter
Splutter gutter.

Mind reader

Octopus oats
Hamster hops
Gold bold
Icy slicey
Perfect pancake
Bake shake.

Olivia Hodges (9)
St Michael's Preparatory School, Leigh-on-Sea

The Witches Of Dundee

The witches of Dundee
Have big, black cats
Long, crooked noses
And tall, dark hats.

Moonlit, ugly faces
Show hints of glee,
Witches laugh as they race
From tree to tree.

Witches hoot with laughter
And purring cats
Oh, they purr so loudly
As they smell rats.

Witches are immortal
So they don't die
They just fly above trees
Up in the sky.

Anika Patel (9)
St Michael's Preparatory School, Leigh-on-Sea

Janitor Jeffries

Janitor Jeffries
Scrubs all day
Polish
Wipe
Mops with bucket.

Janitor Jeffries
Cleans tiles,
Windows,
Steps.

Janitor Jeffries
Cleans all night
Until the stars
Come out.

Janitor Jeffries
Very very tired
Bed, bed,
Snore, snore.

Harri-Anne Marsden (8)
St Teresa's RC Primary School, Basildon

Tear Down The City

Down in Scotland out comes Nessie
Down in the North Pole out comes the abominable snowman
Down in Aussie out comes Biggy.
Although Biggy's really called Big Foot
I'll call him Biggy because it rhymes with Nessie
Who lives in a lochie, a lochie called Loch Ness
You guessed he's the Loch Ness Monster.
Nessie destroys the town of Loch Ness
And Snowy destroys Santa's house
And Biggy destroys Sydney.
Then they all sleep for one hundred years.

Robert Smith (8)
St Teresa's RC Primary School, Basildon

Best Friend

B est friend, best friend
E veryone loves best friends
S tay together forever
T ry to make up when we break up

F riend, friend we all have friends
R ight, right your friends are always right
I n the town when you are down your friends
E ven go shopping with you
N ever be down I mean,
D own
S ola is my best friend, do you have one?

Loren Campbell (9)
St Teresa's RC Primary School, Basildon

My Friends

I have this friend,
She lives around the bend!
Her name is Carrie,
Her boyfriend's name is Larry!
She broke her wrist,
By falling over in the mist!

I have this mate,
Her age is eight!
Her name is Michelle,
She lives in a shell!
Her country is Ireland,
But she visits the Canary Islands!

Coral Witherspoon (10)
St Teresa's RC Primary School, Basildon

Snow

Snow is white
It is fun to play with
Snow it is everywhere
And is as cold as ice

Snowman in one big line
Children are playing
Because school is closed
In the morning the snow is gone.

Matthew Thompson (10)
St Teresa's RC Primary School, Basildon

Soft Toys

I have a nice soft toy
Well, it is a boy.
He is a teddy bear
I go with him everywhere.
I play with him up in my room
And put him on the broom.
I take him for a ride
And say, his name is Clyde.

Jeanette Harrigan (10)
St Teresa's RC Primary School, Basildon

Bananas

Monkeys hanging in a tree
Jumping up and being free,
Who could all these monkeys be?
No bananas left for you or me.

Monkeys singing la di da,
Monkeys driving in a car,
Monkeys are who they are,
Hanging round a drinking bar.

Janine Powell (10)
St Teresa's RC Primary School, Basildon

School Sucks

School, school, don't tell me about it
Because I hate it,
Handwriting, history, literacy and numeracy
DT and art don't forget about draft, ICT and
Science, don't forget about RE.
The only thing I like about school is PE.
My brother thinks school's cool,
I'd think I'd rather swim in a pool,
But the only things that make school exciting
are my friends.

Leah Langley (9)
St Teresa's RC Primary School, Basildon

A Snow Poem

Snow, snow I love snow,
Blows through the breezy night.
Snow snow I love snow
If I'm lucky, it just might glow.
In the snow you must wear gloves,
Sometimes people see the doves.

If you see ice
You barely see mice.
Even when they're nice.
Ice, ice, it don't taste like rice, or roll like a dice
Ice, ice, I really love ice.

Cherise Breward (9)
St Teresa's RC Primary School, Basildon

Stane's Magic Wand

'It really will work,' said Jack yesterday
Just as our teacher was clearing away,
'If I wave this wand and say the right words,
That pile of Mass books will turn into birds.'
Our teacher became the most elegant pig
Wearing his trotters and dancing a gig.
Ms Brown grew a beard,
Ms Green turned red with the caretaker's mop
Stuck on her head.
I got it from my Uncle Stan such an amazing, mysterious man.

Melissa Kelly (9)
St Teresa's RC Primary School, Basildon

The Bogalogalol

The Bogalogalol is evil,
He eats lots of people,
It's very simple,
He'll give you a ghostly pimple,
You won't dare to fight,
Unless you're a knight,
He's as big as King Kong,
And very strong.
You'll hear him groan,
He'll step on your phone,
Not to mention your house,
You'll look like a mouse,
He'll eat your chocolate cake,
And he's *not fake!*

Shane Thorn (10)
St Teresa's RC Primary School, Basildon

What Am I?

People walk through me
And I am brown and tall
Who am I?

I am white
And people write,
Draw and colour me
Who am I?

People read me
And borrow me
From a library
Who am I?

People should hold me
Shake me
And keep me
Who am I?

Samantha Hand (10)
St Teresa's RC Primary School, Basildon

A Wonderful Summer

Sunshine all around me
But mostly I sit under a tree
We always get out the pool
I would rather stay home than
School.

Sunshine all around me
My best friend's Dad is Lee.
My friends come, we have a water fight
Sometimes my friends stay the night.

Sunshine all around me
One of the boys is horrible isn't he.
Sunshine, sunshine, shining so bright,
Sometimes I wish the night had some light.

Emma Viner (9)
St Teresa's RC Primary School, Basildon

A Poem About Snow

Snow is white,
It falls down like a kite.
Snow is cold,
It tastes like mould.
Snow is shining like a crystal,
It looks like a water pistol.

Snow is falling all around me,
It falls on me - could it be
Snow falls on the cars,
It shines like stars.
Snow is cold just like ice,
People sit indoors and play a board game with dice.

Lyndsey Roberts (9)
St Teresa's RC Primary School, Basildon

Iced Ink - The Punk Skunk's Song

If you like to whiff and if you like to reek after me shout out,
'Iced ink.'

If you like to stink and smell after me shout out, 'Iced ink.'

If you like to smell like a pair of socks that reek after me
shout out, 'Iced ink.'

If you have dirt stinking on your clothes after me shout out,
'Iced Ink.'

If you like to pong and whiff after me shout out,
'Iced Ink.'

Lillian Smith (7)
St Teresa's RC Primary School, Basildon

Iced Ink Punk Skunk's Song

Stinky smelly
Just like jelly
Wobble, wobble, stinky
Whiff, smelly socks
Wobble, stinky jelly
Just like a flat tyre.

Bananas smell just like old gel,
Smelly dirt on my shirt
Pooey now that smells.

Smelly sausages are horrible
Sometimes I put my hand on my nose
Because it really stinks.

When people come in round my house
They go in my fridge
They say that stinks
No one has come round my house since.

Blayne Cronin (7)
St Teresa's RC Primary School, Basildon

Friendship

F riends, friends
R each out for you
 I n every way, whenever you are feeling blue
E ven when you have a fall out
N ever go on your own about
D o you want to be my best friend?
S hall we go round the bend?
H elen said 'Yes' it's because
 I am totally the best
P lease be my friend.

Sola Ekosanmi (9)
St Teresa's RC Primary School, Basildon

Iced Ink Punk Skunk Song

Sing a punk skunk song
If you like to stink like a pair of socks that are pink
No wonder that they smell they have been cast by
a magic spell
If you smell a funny whiff just jump off a cliff.

Do you smell a funny smell from your nostril?
Then it must be really impossible
I have not washed my socks all week
Now they smell like beetroot and leek
I smell a funny pong but can you still sing the
Punk skunk song?

Please put them in the washing machine
Then they will be nice and clean
I still smell a funny stink,
Come on altogether shout out Iced Ink.

Andrew Baker (8)
St Teresa's RC Primary School, Basildon

The Dark Avenger

My dog is called Josie
Hello I'm Josie.

She does everything I say
Yes I do.

She runs about when I take her for a walk.
Woof! Woof! Woof!

When she sleeps she is loud
Sh sh sh sh sh!

She likes to splash in puddles
Splash! Splash!

There is a pale dog ahead of us
A greyhound from over the road.

Marie Anderson (8)
St Teresa's RC Primary School, Basildon

My Dog Truedy

My dog is called Truedy
Hello friend I'm Gemma.

She understands every word I say
Come on
'Woof! Woof! Woooo!'

Sometimes I take her for a walk she loves it
'Yippee I love walks, woof!'

She always stays in front of me just in case
'I always pull her along behind me.'

Sometimes I check to see if she is OK.
'Woof!'

She sniffs every time she stops.
'Woof! Woof!'

Alex Metcalfe (8)
St Teresa's RC Primary School, Basildon

A Pirate's Life

Oh a pirate's life is a wonderful life
To sail the seven seas.
Time flies by as you look at the sky.
A storm comes round and roars like a pound.
The boat won't float and again and again
Sinks a little bit more.
Up, up and down, down
I look like a clown
With seaweed all over my face.
An island nearby, is it real?
Listen 'ere sea, make a deal
If you push me there, I leave you I swear.
I touch the sand with my crumpled up hand
A pirate's life.

Leanne Dodd (8)
St Teresa's RC Primary School, Basildon

Janitor Jeffries

Janitor Jeffries
Sad again
Washing and scrubbing
All day again
He must be tired
Now he must get to bed when the work is done.

Janitor Jeffries
Up right now
Mopping and scrubbing
Upstairs and down
Working all day and to midnight
Now he is going on holiday.

Janitor Jeffries
Having an ice cream
He is enjoying it lots
Because it is strawberry
Now he is swimming backwards and forwards
He is a good swimmer too.

Janitor Jeffries
Home again
Scrubbing and soaking
All day and to midnight.

Raeanne Beckwith (8)
St Teresa's RC Primary School, Basildon

My Little Sister

My little sister is a pain in the bum
When she is naughty I tell my mum
My little sister sometimes makes me sad
When she does I tell my dad
She makes me laugh when she sings
But I wouldn't change her for anything.

Charlotte Bettle (9)
St Teresa's RC Primary School, Basildon

Janitor Jeffries

Janitor Jeffries
Cleaning all day
Scrubbing
Wiping.

Janitor Jeffries
Playing all day
Breaking
Putting away.

Janitor Jeffries
Scrubbing all night
Polishing
Cleaning
Wiping.

Janitor Jeffries
Going to bed
Sleeping
Snoring
Nice dreams
Tonight.

Faye Corrigan (7)
St Teresa's RC Primary School, Basildon

Jellyfish

Jellyfish
Sting its prey
Big, soft, stretchy,
Like a mite in the water.
Like a live flower in the night
Makes me feel strong
As small as their prey.

Jellyfish
Makes me remember the first time
I fished in a river
It is special to me.

Peter Murray (10)
St Teresa's RC Primary School, Basildon

O God I Love You

O God, O God, I love You
O God, O God, I love You
You are the best, You are so great
You love everyone.
It is too much the love You give to us.
It is so kind of You.
We love You so much.
We can't let You leave.

Katie Carter (9)
St Teresa's RC Primary School, Basildon

Bonfire For The Fish

Fish looking up there
High in the sky
Bonfire shining
Twinkling in my eye
I feel so low I *am* so low
What is that? What is that glow?
I see it falling in the pond.
Thank you light for the bonfire.

Annabelle Bottjer (8)
St Teresa's RC Primary School, Basildon

Fairy Dance

Dance along as the fairies sing
Twirl around in a ring.
Do the stuff that the fairies do.
Dance like the fairies do.
Just believe in fairies
And you're a fairy.

Ellis Keogh (8)
St Teresa's RC Primary School, Basildon

Times Tables

1 x 1 = 1 don't you think that's fun?
1 x 2 = 2 finally we got through
1 x 3 = 3 do you want to work with me?
1 x 4 = 4 shall we do some more?
1 x 5 = 5 shall we have a jive?
1 x 6 = 6 shall we do a mix?
1 x 7 = 7 shall we count to eleven?
1 x 8 = 8 do you want to be my mate?
1 x 9 = 9 hey that book's mine
1 x 10 = 10 shall we do that again?
1 x 11 = 11 shall we go to Devon
1 x 12 = 12 I wish I was an elf.

Clare Hobday (8)
St Teresa's RC Primary School, Basildon

Leaves

L eaves fall from the ground
E agles fly south
A ll swans fly south
V ultures too
E veryone celebrates
S outh is the way all birds fly.

Jamie Cook (9)
St Teresa's RC Primary School, Basildon

Shine Stars

S hine in the night
T eachers have tea
A little girl goes in at night
R ight now go to bed
S leep tight, night, night Mum.

Stevie Smith (8)
St Teresa's RC Primary School, Basildon

Children Playing

C hildren get excited about autumn
H opping in the leaves
I nside their mums washing and cleaning
L oving the leaves so much they're
D ancing about
R eaching for non-falling leaves
E agles fly south
N ot even getting a stitch.

P eeking at everyone else
L oving the
A nimals
Y ippee!
I nside their dads are sleeping
N ot even watching the children
G ood children playing.

Henry Green (8)
St Teresa's RC Primary School, Basildon

Hibernation

As animals go to their nest to sleep
I'll be indoors all wrapped up in bed.
Maybe I need a hot water bottle,
Or two quilts to keep me warm.
Lots of hot mugs of sweet tea.
Golden leaves fall to the ground.
Otters go to hibernate in the bushes
Or catch their food to eat in spring.
Sleeping from autumn and sleep to spring.
Little animals are not in sight.
Even birds fly south,
Except robins.
He gives a painful warning sound.

Shannon Thorn (8)
St Teresa's RC Primary School, Basildon

Fairy Dancing

Fairy dancing is so sweet
They sing and sing till the bells of the church ring.
Then they hide away.
The afternoon's gone, the sun's disappeared
Then they jump up and start singing again.
Autumn has gone, fairies stay in the bushes all day.
The wind is strong,
The wind is cold, it's snowing
And snowing it never stops.

Laura Broomfield (9)
St Teresa's RC Primary School, Basildon

The Sea Is Flowing

The sea is flowing all day long
Because the wind is blowing strong.
The waves are clashing
And the clouds are bashing,
And it's making a terrible bang.
Up and down all around the town just
to see the clown
But when the tide comes in
Everyone wants a swim.
Bye-bye water,
Bye-bye sea,
Bye-bye everything,
Bye-bye me.
Now everything is gone,
It's been gone for so long.

Katie Maginn (8)
St Teresa's RC Primary School, Basildon

Holidays

Go to France
Go in a cab
Go to the beach
And catch some crabs.

Go to Spain
Go on a train
Go to the shops
And there is rain.

Lois Blackman (8)
St Teresa's RC Primary School, Basildon

Orlando

O utstanding is he
R omeo to me
L oving him is my thing
A nd Orlando is definitely my *King!*
N ice is not the name for my love
D arling Orlando can I be your lady dove?
O h, how I love you Orlando Bloom.

Connie Meddle (9)
St Teresa's RC Primary School, Basildon

Poem On Autumn

L ead the church
E at the food
A mber light shines
V ery bright
E venings by the fire
S ee this food nice and warm.

Sharon Madziva (8)
St Teresa's RC Primary School, Basildon

Poem On Autumn

L eaves fall down all around
E very bird flies south
A ll leaves turn orange when they fall, they have
V ery pretty colours
E veryone loves autumn because the leaves fall
S mall creatures make homes under leaves.

Elisha Dudfield (8)
St Teresa's RC Primary School, Basildon

Animals

A s the leaves fall down
N ow they are different colours
I n our home we have hot chocolate
M making lots of piles of leaves
A s all the birds fly south
playing in the
L eaves is fun,
the
S ummer sun has gone away
autumn is here today.

Jordan Brown (8)
St Teresa's RC Primary School, Basildon

Sunrise

The sunrise
Rises at dawn
Colourful, bright, wonderful
Like new fire
Like new wallpaper
The sunrise
Reminds us of the new day.

Akanki Baptiste (11)
St Teresa's RC Primary School, Basildon

Summer Has Gone

S ummer has gone
U nder the ground the
M oles are cold
M others bake cookies
    I am
E ating up the cookies
R eally nice

S ome animals hibernate
O n the floor brown leaves. September,
O ctober and
N ovember are autumn months.

Joseph Wilson (9)
St Teresa's RC Primary School, Basildon

Maths

One, two, who are you?
Three, four, do some more.
Five, six, do some tricks.
Seven, eight, work with a mate.
Nine, ten, don't use a pen.
Eleven, twelve, have a delve.
Thirteen, fourteen, don't be so mean.
    You've finished
    Your maths
    Finally!

Natasha Magnus (8)
St Teresa's RC Primary School, Basildon

Extinction

Many animals face extinction
From the lion to the whale,
And if you think you cannot help,
You can, so don't fail.

The lion is a vicious predator,
Eating meat every day,
With a golden mane,
So help them as I say.

The whale is a large mammal
They mostly eat krill,
Heavier than thirty elephants,
So help them, if you will.

Giant turtles are endangered too,
Large and slow as they
Relax all day, without a care,
So help them, today!

A white rhino roams 'round free,
Without a care in the world
Hunted for their horns,
At them bullets are hurled.

Elephants are heavy and large
Cleaning in watering holes,
Herbivores are they,
Veg they eat, not young foals.

Eagles fly about free,
Endangered are they,
One of the birds of Scotland,
So stop shooting them, this day.

With an orange fur coat,
And black stripes, the tigers
Do not fight,
They live where there are no bikers.

The ostrich is a very large bird,
Laying giant eggs.
No doubt they can run fast,
With their pink long legs.

Dolphins swim in the sea today
Endangered because of fishermen's nets,
Silky skin they have,
So help them, lets.

Animals are important
To our every day life.
So don't harm them,
Especially with a knife.

Luke Matthews (11)
St Teresa's RC Primary School, Basildon

The Waterfall

The waterfall,
With smooth glistening water,
Like a straight piece of glass,
Like a sheet of blue paper falling down,
Like hundreds of spheres falling down,
It makes me feel peaceful,
Like forever silence,
The waterfall,
Reminds us that life never stops.

Liam Brine (11)
St Teresa's RC Primary School, Basildon

The Dinosaur

With long, sharp claws
Gigantic, vicious, loud,
Like a lizard
Like a big blizzard
Something that makes me feel small
Like a beetle on a log
The dinosaur
Reminds me how precious life is.

Elliott Tyner (11)
St Teresa's RC Primary School, Basildon

Dolphin

The dolphin
it eats fish,
big, smooth, grey or blue.
As clear as a calculator
as blue as the sea it's living in.
It makes me feel I have smooth skin.
it makes me feel as small as its food.
The dolphin,
dolphins are wonderful and would
save you from drowning so they
shouldn't be hunted down.

Georgina Parker (11)
St Teresa's RC Primary School, Basildon

The Rainbow

The rainbow
Is very colourful
Soft, beautiful, arch-shaped
Like a bridge across the sky
Like a precious diamond
It makes me feel delicate
Like a red rose
The rainbow
Reminds me life is wonderful.

Paige McGuigan (11)
St Teresa's RC Primary School, Basildon

The Pencil

The pencil
Used for writing and was used on this paper
Small, colourless, useful
Like a stamp on printer paper
Like a chopstick which has been in cement
It makes me feel big
Like a giant which no one is scared of
The pencil
Reminds me that the more you write the shorter it seems!

George Green (10)
St Teresa's RC Primary School, Basildon

The Ocean

The ocean can be shining blue
Bright as the sky
Sparkling with joy.

Appreciate the ocean as it is now
Dirty, murky, misty and grey,
You are creating pollution.

Please protect the ocean!

Natasha Blay (11)
St Teresa's RC Primary School, Basildon

A Friend

A friend
Kind and generous
Loves, cares, and is there for you.
Funny and great to be around,
Makes me feel so loved and cared for
A friend.
Makes me think of my family
Friends are special and care for each other.

Lacey Dunmow (11)
St Teresa's RC Primary School, Basildon

Monkey

Monkey, monkey, up in a tree,
Running around and shouting with glee.
You're having fun, and eating bananas
Laughing at people in pink pyjamas,
Oh I wish I was you, silly monkey,
So I can run and laugh with thee.

You're fast, you're little and quick and brown,
Running around like a little clown,
If I were you I would go coo, coo,
Dear little monkey, I wish I were you.
I would run around and disappear in a single bound,
Little, brown monkey, don't make a sound.

Levi Al Blackman (11)
St Teresa's RC Primary School, Basildon

The Rivers

You are crystal blue,
You are crystal clear,
We admire you,
You sparkle when we're near.

You give us water to drink,
In you we have bathed,
We use you in our sinks,
But you need to be saved.

We dump our waste in you,
And we don't even care,
Carelessly we fish in you,
Until there is nothing to spare.

If we do not do something soon,
Then you will be gone,
All the rivers and lagoons,
Something must be done.

David Odejayi (10)
St Teresa's RC Primary School, Basildon

Dolphins And Humans

Dolphins are good
Humans are bad.

Dolphins are sad
Humans are mad.

Dolphins are magnificent creatures
They live in features.

They love all creatures
Even the teachers.

Scott Irving (11)
St Teresa's RC Primary School, Basildon

What's Wrong With The World?

What's wrong with the world?
What's happening today?
What's wrong with our planet
That we live on each day?
Why are our animals endangered and harmed?
Answer me the question, I need to know.
Why do we fish
For fun and food?
Why don't we be vegetarians?
But what would we eat if we did not fish?
A piece of fruit, or maybe some cheese
How thin will we get if we don't eat?
I do not know, and do not care.
What's wrong with *our* world today?
What's wrong with our world?

Mary-Ann Iyiola (10)
St Teresa's RC Primary School, Basildon

The Elephant

The elephant
Roams around in herds,
Enormous, endangered, powerful,
As big as a double-decker bus.
As powerful as a bulldozer
Makes me feel small,
As small as an ant.
The elephant
I am not the most important
Person on
Earth.

Daniel Fife (11)
St Teresa's RC Primary School, Basildon

The Willow Tree

The willow tree,
So very helpless,
Strong, tall, towering,
Like buildings reaching for the sky,
And like old houses being knocked down.
It makes me feel short,
Like a mouse to a man.
The willow tree,
It reminds me that humans are not always the
most important beings.

Thomas Bottjer (11)
St Teresa's RC Primary School, Basildon

The Dolphin

The dolphin
A magnificent, unique creature.
Swims in mystical water
At sunrise the sun glistens
Off the still wavy seas
As the glamorous shining moon kisses
The water.
Dolphins, soft glistening features
Blink in the moonlight
As they leap out of the water.

Dolphins are such wonderful creatures
I wish I was one.

Adetayo Davies (10)
St Teresa's RC Primary School, Basildon

The Digger

The digger,
Attracted by the convent,
Destructive, mighty, huge
Like a giant hand picking up some dirt,
Like a small person being crushed by a
giant arm.
It makes me feel afraid,
Like a monster destroying anything in its way.
The digger
Reminds us how weak we are.

Sean Malone (10)
St Teresa's RC Primary School, Basildon

If I Was A Whale

If I was a whale I would swim with the other fish,
I would eat the krill,
I would launch off into the air
And crash back down into the sea.
I would be as loud as an aeroplane,
And hurt human's ears.
If I was a whale.

Danny Moss (11)
St Teresa's RC Primary School, Basildon

My Shed

I don't go into my shed on my own
I never know what I might find
It's dark there and gloomy and full of weird stuff,
Of every imaginable kind.

I don't go into my shed on my own
There's boxes of beasts that aren't nice
I've heard them all scratching and scurrying about
Though Dad says it's just a few mice.

I don't go into my shed on my own
There's wood there, once part of a boat
And a big grizzly bear with enormous sharp teeth
Though Mum says it's just a fur coat.

I don't go into my shed on my own
I'm a baby I admit it, it's true
But then if I asked you to go there alone
Be honest and truthful, would you?

Kirsty Byram (11)
Stambridge Primary School

Fairies As Friends

Some people say I'm silly because
I believe in fairies
But I'll tell you something
Fairies are my friends.

They come in through the window and
Chat to me at night.

My other friends think it is out
Of the ordinary
But I think it's extraordinary
To have
Fairies as friends.

Aliesha Booth (8)
Stambridge Primary School

Christmas

Christmas is soon
It's beginning to snow
And children's small noses
Are starting to glow.

Their faces are shining
With hope and with glee
As they all decorate
The huge Christmas tree.

They have written their letters
Now they hope and they pray
That they get what they want
To open on Christmas Day.

Katy Byram (8)
Stambridge Primary School

About My Friend

She's my friend, yes she's my friend.
I really do recommend.
She helped me through good and bad
And made me laugh when I was sad.
She's normally quick and on the run,
Although that happens she still is fun.
She has got such lovely hair,
But sometimes doesn't play fair.
She's pretty and very sweet,
Although she has smelly feet.
I know this because she stayed the night,
I could smell them and they gave me a
fright.
Even through that, she's still my friend,
Yes, still my friend,
I really do recommend.

Lisa Martin (10)
Thorpedene Junior School

Odd Boys!

There are some odd boys in our school,
Like Mike is mistaken for a fool.
His best friend who is John Green,
Whose arms are made of plasticine.
Max has a head made of balloon,
Which he hopes to get rid of soon.
There is a boy full of straw,
He seems to be getting more and more!
Another boy is made of rock,
And sometimes wears a frilly frock!

Roberta Chaplin (10)
Thorpedene Junior School

The Perfect Couple

Here comes the bride,
Big, fat and wide,
Nice rotten teeth, in a
Smile filled with pride.

Huge goggly eyes,
Great wobbly thighs,
Long matted hair and the
Scent of pigstys.

Here comes the groom,
Fresh from the tomb,
Shuffling along with a
Look full of gloom.

Skin grey and dank,
Hair long and lank,
A face that is crumbling and
Stench rather rank.

Oh, what a pair,
Folk stop and stare,
Brave ones take photos but
Just for a dare!

So, you may weep,
Your flesh may creep,
But it just proves
Beauty's only skin deep!

Leeanne Palmer (11)
Thorpedene Junior School

Clock

I am a face that ticks till I stop,
I can count till twelve but I shine till night.
I have got two ears rather large but,
I have got twelve eyes all over the face,
But my nose is all over the place,

And I scream when you tell me to!

(I'm a clock)

Ellie Townley (8)
Thorpedene Junior School

Mars

I went to the planet Mars
And rode on all the stars
It was very sunny
But not very funny
So I went to this strange planet
And met an alien called Janet
Who had a wriggly nose
And lots of crooked toes
Or the other way around who knows?
So that was that
But the alien still thought I was a brat.

Charlotte Townley (9)
Thorpedene Junior School